YOU'RE MOVING WHERE?

By
Theodore Potter

PotterHouse Publishing LLC
Tok, Alaska 99780

The life story of a country music singer from birth to present day, singing through the Army, Australia, and the United States.

All Rights Reserved
No part of this book may be reproduced, scanned, or distributed in any printed or electronic form without permission. Please do not participate in or encourage piracy of copyrighted materials in violation of author's rights. Purchase only authorized editions.
For information, email the author at potterlwen@hotmail.com

Copyright © 2012 Theodore Potter
All rights reserved.
ISBN: 978-0-9799567-3-7

DEDICATION

For Fern, My loving and talented wife.

CHAPTER 1

In December of nineteen forty five, three things happened of concern in Macon county Georgia. One, World War Two ended shortly after Hitler committed suicide in his bunker and the rest of the bad guys of the world, saw merit in not making War, against a country that would drop a bomb on their butts to stop their world domination attempts.

Next, upon his release from active Army service, Diller Clark Fargo, married Ruby Darby and, impregnated her. Nine months later to the day, Clark Donald Fargo came into this world and as he did, he let go with a blood curdling yell, causing the entire staff of the small Macon hospital to cringe. This boy had one powerful set of lungs that literally set one's nerve ends on a cutting edge.

No Father on the face of earth was more proud of a son than Diller was of Clark. He absolutely adored the child from the moment he first held him and the two were almost inseparable. Diller missed his offspring when he was away at work, and didn't much care for work anyhow, so a lot of times Diller just stayed home and looked after his son, and Ruby went to work as a waitress, supporting the three of them.

A consequence of this was that Clark grew up poor, but he didn't notice, except at school. He learned early on to let the insults roll off his back like water ran off a well waxed car hood. He never had to work very hard to bring a presentable report card home either.

Clark's best subject in school was music. He had a clear sweet voice the Teacher loved, and was quick to pick up on music in general. The only thing they clashed over was him not sounding the same as all the other kids. She knew this boy had his own style and was far more talented than most others, so she in general let him have his way. He wanted to play the bass guitar, because he liked the deep sounds the instrument emitted, and could be heard for blocks around.

Clark talked his parents into buying him a Beatle Bass. It was an acoustic hollow body and the great thing was he didn't need an amp to play it through. Clark played forty-five records of popular country songs, in his room at night after school and his favorite was Hank Williams songs.

YOU'RE MOVING WHERE?

The first song he learned to play Bass and sing with was "Your Cheating Heart." He finally got the nerve up to play and sing for his music class at school. A pen falling on the floor would have made an audible sound while Clark performed. When he finished his song, his fellow classmates stood and clapped. Those fellow students, without realizing it, convicted Clark to a life of pain and joy as a country music singer.

Clark had a gift and put it to good use around Macon Georgia. By the time he turned eighteen, he had a good following and a lot of them were female, so Clark wasn't lonesome. He grew into a six foot three inch hunk of a man that most girls wanted to cuddle anyhow.

Clark didn't know it, but his life as a musician caused Ruby and Diller much stress. They didn't mind him playing music, but they weren't getting any sleep on the three or four nights he did each week. Clark came home in the wee morning hours and fell in bed without realizing his mom and dad had not gone to sleep all night, but still had to get up at the normal hour to get things done in their life.

Finally it all came to a head shortly after Clark's eighteenth birthday, Diller and Ruby called a meeting. They got Clark out of bed at the ungodly hour of seven in the morning. Diller asks his son if he was tired. Clark looked at his dad through blood shot eyes that looked like two pee holes in a snow bank, and said. "What do you think Dad; I just got in bed two hours ago."

Diller was silent for a while, then, he quietly said. "So did your mother and I son, each night you stay out, we don't get any sleep, just like you didn't get any last night."

Clark sat there in horrible shock. He was killing his folks for heaven's sake, how could he be so stupid? He apologized to his Dad and Mom and promised he would come up with a solution and fast, and now, could he go back to bed please? They laughed and told him of course.

Clark decided to find someplace else to live. He jumped in his truck and went to some friends place, he told them what happened, and no, they didn't know of any place to rent, but he was welcome to crash here. Clark didn't think he should do that. He needed a real place to live. Back in the truck, he canvassed the town for the next four hours and got nothing whatsoever for his efforts.

As he turned for home, he saw a red sign on the other side of a large open field. He turned left at the next street and drove to the street he had seen the sign on and turned left on to it. The sign was tacked on an apartment above a garage that was separated from a large single story

YOU'RE MOVING WHERE?

white house. The place had the look of a farm house and in fact had been at one time years ago. The sign read for rent, and in small print read, apply at house.

Clark parked his truck on the street, and got out. It was so quiet he could hear the birds tweeting. He walked to the house, went up and rang a bell. He could hear slow footsteps approaching the door. When the door opened he saw an older woman with a full apron. Her hair was done up in a nice way, he said. "Hello, I would like to look at the apartment you have for rent."

The old lady replied with. "Just a moment, let me get my granddaughter, she will show it to you."

Clark was a shy lad, and simply said "OK."

A beautiful young girl came to the door. She said. "Hello, my name is Shelly, What's yours?"

Now Clark had been shy with the old lady, but this lovely person made his tongue tie up in knots. He grew red in the face and couldn't possibly say a word. The girl took pity on him and said. "Oh, come on, I'll show you the apartment."

She walked past him and the wonderful smell of her was almost more than his weakened heart could stand. When she said, "Come on", little did she realize Clark would have followed her over a cliff at this point.

He followed the tantalizing smell of her and watched her bottom swing from side to side. He had to look away. He didn't want this girl to think him a pervert or something. She kept up a steady stream of words as she walked. He couldn't remember one thing she said later on.

She started up the outside stair to the apartment and suddenly her backside was level with his eyes, and he felt like he was going to strangle. He stopped and looked down until she reached the top, then while she was unlocking the door he caught up with her. Shelly looked at him with a strange expression on her face. She said. "I hope you like it; I think you're a nice person."

Clark felt like she had given him the best complement of his life. The apartment was neat as it could be, and filled with quality furnishings throughout. Clark thought this has to be beyond my means. He asked, "What does this rent for?"

Shelly said. "One twenty five a month, but less if you do some chores for my Gran from time to time. I'm in my last year of high school and then I'm off to university up in Columbus this fall. I need someone who will look in on Gran from time to time, could you do that?"

YOU'RE MOVING WHERE?

Clark couldn't believe his luck. He said. "If you will have me, I'll take it and pay in advance right now."

Shelly held up her hands and said, "Let's talk to Gran before a final decision is made."

Shelly was finding herself strongly attracted to this person, and couldn't help herself any more then Clark could. The two went out on the landing and down the stair.

As the two were descending the stair they were being observed by Shelly's Grandmother, standing in her living room looking out the side window. Their body english told her volumes. These two fit together like steak and sauce. She thought, well that's that. She loved her only grandchild so very much, and worried what would happen to her if she was to die.

Shelly was the only child from her son, who died on the beach at Normandy, in that terrible war. The mother had married another and moved out of state. When Ellie's husband died in nineteen fifty two, Shelly's mother brought Shelly to her grandfather's funeral and her mother got Ellie aside, and told her she was dying of cancer and Shelly needed her Grandmother.

Ellie was devastated and agreed to take Shelly and would even help her ex- daughter- in- law if she could. Things had worked out so Shelly could spend time with her mother until the end. Ellie had been there too. It had been hard, and Ellie and the girl had bonded.

That was ten years ago now, and Shelly was eighteen and graduating from high school in a few days, then going off to university and she would be all alone. The two entered the house and Shelly introduced him to Ellie and exclaimed, "He likes it Gran, and he is willing to work some of the rent off."

Ellie knew all was lost now. Her grandchild had found her knight in shining armor, but she still had to go through the motions, for her own sake. She asked, "How old are you son?"

Clark said. "I'm almost nineteen, I graduated high school this year."

She asked him, "Where do you work?"

He said, "I'll be working out at the lumber yard come fall I think."

He didn't think it prudent to tell them about his musical vocation, just yet. One thing he knew for sure was, folks who didn't do music, classed all musicians, in the wanta be musician category. Ellie made up her mind, he seemed like a nice boy and Shelly had good taste in people.

Shelly was all smiles as Clark took money out to pay Ellie, who said, "We'll do all that later, right now, you two look starved to death and I've got a cure for that. I cooked a pot roast with all

YOU'RE MOVING WHERE?

the fixings in my slow cooker and it's ready to eat and I won't take no for an answer."

Ellie wasn't one to argue with, so they sat down and ate, and it was one the most delicious meals he had ever eaten and he told her so.

Clark took off after the meal. He and Shelly exchanged a long look at the door. Clark's heart was racing; he dropped his eyes first, and could feel her eye's on him all the way to the truck. He didn't dare look at her as he drove away.

Clark couldn't believe how lucky he had just been. A great place to live and man Shelly; just thinking about her made his heart beat faster.

Clark had a mess on his hands when he told his parents what he did. Ruby broke out in tears and got incensed at Diller for throwing her baby boy out on the street, Diller defended himself by saying. "You were the one who said you couldn't sleep with your son gone, woman. What did you expect him to do? Give up music? Ha! I don't think so; he's too damn good for that."

Clark stepped in and told the both of them they were taking this the wrong way. It was time he got on his own anyhow, and the two needed their sleep at night. This calmed the two down and Clark began packing the truck with his belongings. His dad helped and his mother put a bunch of stuff from all over the house and kitchen in as well. Her son would be able to cook and eat off plates by golly. He told his dad and mom to follow him over and meet his land lady and her granddaughter, Ruby's heart froze. She knew the girl was the key to the lock, in this whole thing.

When the Fargo family arrived at Clark's new place, Ellie made them feel so welcome, that Ruby forgot all about her feelings of losing her son. She and Diller fell in love with Shelly. She thought it would be a good thing if Shelly and Clark became a couple. After coffee and cake, Ruby said. "I would love to see your new apartment son."

Clark said. "Come on mom and dad I'll show you my place."

Clark and his dad carted all his junk up the stair case, it took many trips and the two were bushed when the truck was cleaned out. Clark still had his music gear back home. When the visiting drew to a close, Clark drove to his parent's home, with them trailing behind.

CHAPTER 2
LEARNING THE BUSINESS

Clark and his band worked a three night a week gig out on the bypass at the Holiday Inn. Clark and Two Plus One Country group, played Thursday, Friday and Saturday nights. The Band consisted of Brad Johns on lead and Doc Saunders, on rhythm guitar.

The three had played together since Clark had got up in front of them and played "Your Cheating Heart" way back in grade school, and had remained the best of friends. The gig paid them well for the area. Clark received the lion's share of the two hundred bucks they received each night they played, Brad and Doc got fifty-five dollars each and were happy to get it. Clark had gotten the gig and bought the PA system and did all the singing. He received ninety bucks for his effort. The gig wasn't the only work they did. A couple of times a month Clark booked them into a dance hall on Saturday night, letting someone else play the Holiday Inn gig. He made a deal with the alternate band to keep it country.

The dances the guys played, were for the most part, wild uninhibited barely controlled free for alls. The worst was Rains Ball Room in Columbus Georgia. The time they played it, some guy with only one leg on crutches, became upset because he wasn't able to find a partner to dance to Clark's music. He dropped one of his crutches, and then taking the other by the small end, he begins swinging it in a wide arc cursing at everyone. The music stopped, and the crowd backed away from him. He soon wore out and never hit anyone. He sank to the hardwood floor, and put his head in his hands, bawling like a baby.

There was dead silence in the huge dance hall. Finally, two cops gently helped the man to his feet, gave him both his crutches, and then escorted him to the exit. Clark said, "Let's play only fast songs for awhile."

They kicked in G and Clark sang, "Take Me Back to Tulsa". The crowd loved it, some local guy jumped on stage with a fiddle and played with them, he wasn't real good, but the locals loved him and the place went wild. They probably did the longest version of the song ever. Clark learned something that night about himself; he could make up new verses in his

YOU'RE MOVING WHERE?

head. The three laughed on the way home. Doc said. "Ninety-nine verses and they still raised the roof when the song finally ended. Boy I call that good. Clark you need to write some songs, you have a knack for it."

Clark packed his music gear up in the truck and parked it in the front drive, went up and flopped on the bed with just a blanket over him. He needed rest in order to play tonight. Little did he know, leaving that music gear in the truck and parking it where Shelly and her grandmother had to look at it all afternoon with conflicting emotions, would cause such a stir. Shelly, for her part loved music, but when Clark mentioned he played guitar, just like everyone else, and was told by someone they played music her reaction was ok, so what.

She went to two or three Concerts a year and just last month she had seen George Jones in concert and last year she and Gran had gone to see Johnny Cash and his Tennessee Three. She liked Clark. If he turned out to be a bad singer, it would bring him down in her eyes, and it hurt her heart and she didn't even understand why. She had only just met him.

Shelly, couldn't take it any longer. At seven o'clock, she knocked on Clark's door. He came to the door still half asleep, but when he saw Shelly he came fully awake. Shelly didn't waste time; she came right to her point. She said. "Why didn't you tell us you were a musician and you played in a band?"

Clark's eyes grew big and he said. "I did tell you Shelly, you just didn't hear me, that's all. I'm sorry you feel this way about it. I have been playing music all my life and I won't stop now. If you're unhappy about renting to me, just give back my money, and I'll be on my way. I will not stay in a place where I'm not totally welcome."

Shelly felt like crying. She had read him wrong. She said. "I'm so sorry, I remember now you saying you played guitar. I feel like a fool. Please don't move out, you are more than welcome here. I apologize."

Shelly had grown red in the face, and then she turned and fled down the stairs. She ran all the way to her bedroom, breaking into tears as soon as she closed her door. Her Gran knew exactly what was going on, her granddaughter was falling in love with Clark and there was nothing she could, or would do about it. She had had a love affair with a music man once, with disastrous results. She would pray for the both of them.

When Clark arrived at the Holiday Inn, Brad and Doc were already there. The two helped Clark bring in and set up the PA system. The guys played for two hours without a break. Clark

YOU'RE MOVING WHERE?

found it hard to get in his normal groove. The other two players felt his discomfort.

At the break, Clark leaned his Bass on his amp, stepped off stage, right into Shelly's arms. He hadn't seen her come in, in the almost dark room. The two waltzed around in each other's arms simply to keep from falling down. The hug lasted longer than it had to. Neither felt like letting go, but Clark let his arms drop first. Shelly spoke first, she said. "Clark I am so sorry for doubting you, I promise, I will never make that mistake again."

Her head was hanging low by the time she finished. Clark stepped up to her, and put his hand under her chin, raised her head until they were looking into each other's eyes. They held gazes for a longtime and both knew there was no going back now. They kissed long and deeply. They were in love now and both happy with each other.

CHAPTER 3

Clark and his band were getting real poplar in a three state area. He was writing some songs now, and for the most part, the songs were getting good reception from the audiences they played for. Shelly was up in Atlanta getting educated. The two joked with one another that, someone had to make a living in their relationship, and they both knew, he could take a million dollars and keep singing till it was all gone.

Shelly lived for the times she could take a break, and come home to Clark and Gran. These two had become very good friends, Clark always checked on her every chance he got. When Shelly came home, Gran insisted the two kids spend most of the time together. She sure was glad she had held her tongue back when they first met. Not only were they a handsome couple, they were smart and didn't rush into things.

YOU'RE MOVING WHERE?

Shelly handled Clark's celebrity status with an outward coolness she didn't always feel inside. She knew women came on to Clark at every show he did, but she trusted him and never let her jealous bone show. Men came on to her all the time at university, the same thing applied, she belonged to Clark, and that's all there was to it.

Clark and his folks actually saw more of each other now than they had when he lived with them. A Sunday dinner turned to tears for Ruby. Clark mentioned he and his band were contemplating a move to Nashville. Ruby and Diller said in unison, "You're moving where?"

Diller said. "Son you have it made here in Macon. You have a good following, and Bass players are as common as chicken squat up in Nashville. Your mother and I hoped you would settle down and raise a family here at home. Now you're leaving and might not come home for years."

When he finished speaking, Ruby let go a howl that sounded like a dying calf in a thunder storm, causing Diller and Clark to look at her in amazement. Clark said. "Now mom, I'm not leaving anytime soon, and I for sure won't go forever. This is my home. When one has talent, one must be in the thick of things, or he won't be noticed. We intend to take our time and not jump, except in the right direction."

Ruby was mollified somewhat, and stopped wailing. Diller was glad, he loved Ruby, but she sure could get on his nerves sometimes, especially when she expressed her emotions vocally.

Clark and Shelly spent the summer of nineteen sixty six together, mostly on the road. Music was treating Clark and Two Plus One Country well. They were packing venues with fans, wherever they played, however Clark realized, they needed to record in order to gain even more popularity. He was planning to do something about that, now they were opening for big names.

Then a bomb shell was dropped on the band. Brad Johns was drafted into the US Army. Vietnam was in full swing, and he was bound to go there. Brad was one year older then Clark and Doc. They would get their notices before Christmas.

After Brad left, they had to break in a new rhythm player. His name was Delbert Quincy and he was told from the start he would replace Brad temporarily. He agreed, and the beat went on.

The draft board for Macon, Georgia, sped its selection up in the fall of 1966 and Clark and

YOU'RE MOVING WHERE?

Doc received their draft notice. Clark talked with Doc and they both agreed they would have a better chance of doing music in the Army if they joined for three years. Clark cancelled all gigs. He talked to his mom and dad about it. Diller was proud of his son for making a smart decision. He knew the Army would more than likely put his son and his band to good use, if he joined, instead of rolling with the flow, allowing himself to be inducted.

The US Army sent Doc and Clark to Fort Hood, near Killeen Texas, for their basic training. The two had joined on the buddy system, and couldn't be separated from each other, except if one of them became incapacitated. They joined up to be tank drivers. The Army had a funny way of turning things around however.

When they reported for basic, they were sent to the combat engineers for six weeks of learning how to soldier. Clark reasoned that he and Doc would be the best soldiers on the Fort Hood base. This would give them a chance at special services and music. When their six weeks were done they were assigned to an Aviation outfit and put to work OJT [on the job training]. The two didn't complain, even if their contract did read tank drivers. Airplanes to the two seemed little friendlier then tanks did.

Theodore Potter

Two weeks later found Doc and Clark on their way to Fort Rucker Alabama, the aviation center for the US Army. When they signed in to Rucker, they were handed orders to proceed on two weeks leave and return to Ft Rucker for mechanics school. The two were jubilant, two weeks at home sounded like heaven right now. They wasted no time getting out of Rucker and on their way home to Macon, Georgia.

Clark and Doc took a Greyhound bus to Macon. Clark called Shelly just before loading and she would be at the depot waiting for them.

Clark and Doc hadn't been this happy since the day before they received their draft notice. They were proud of their uniforms, and caused quite a stir at the bus depot. Their popularity hadn't waned in the six weeks they were gone. The war was an unpopular one and a few hippy types gave them a hard time, but nothing serious. The majority were fans, who cast a shadow over the protesters.

Shelly ran to Clark and jumped into his arms wrapping her legs around his middle. Doc stood there in embarrassment, wishing he had a girl to welcome him home like that. Shelly hugged Doc and said. "I'm so glad to see the both of you."

Doc felt much better after that. They drove Doc to his parent's house and let him off. Clark

YOU'RE MOVING WHERE?

told him. "Bring your ax around in a few days and let's do some music."

Shelly exclaimed. "I almost forgot! The Holiday Inn has been calling me. I think they want you to play while you're home on leave."

Clark asked, "How did they know I was here?"

Shelly said. "They called and asked where you were and I told them you were on your way home."

Clark said. "I'll call Quincy and see if he can do a gig with us."

Clark didn't want to play, but felt obligated to at least check it out. He called the manager at the Inn. The guy was so happy to talk to him, it radiated through the phone. When Clark explained that he really didn't have enough time to get his outfit together, the Manager said. "We'll pay you good money to play one show before you return to duty."

When he told Clark what he would be paid, it almost strangled him. It was more then he made in a year in the Army; he told the guy, "OK, we'll do it."

Next he called his two musicians, and set up a practice session with them.

Clark and Shelly spent two days not seeing anyone but Shelly's Grandmother. The old lady felt like one of her grandsons had come home.

She couldn't do enough for him, and even fixed meals for the both of them. On his third day home, the two young lovers visited with Ruby and Diller.

Diller told his son, he and his mother were thinking about selling the house and buying a camping trailer, then travel around the country. At first Clark was a bit upset that his parents were selling the home he had lived in for eighteen years, but then he realized his home was the Army now and he didn't want to deny his folks the pleasure of travel, so he gave them his blessings.

Clark and Shelly both paid Ellie rent on the apartment, not that Ellie wanted them to. Clark insisted and prevailed. Clark used the garage to park his Chevy truck in while he took basic Training. He was planning on driving it from now on. He and Doc were damn tired of public transportation, and besides they could haul their gear along with them. All they needed was a camper top to keep the stuff secure and dry.

CHAPTER 4
FIRST PAYING CUSTOMERS

Clark couldn't believe what he was seeing. There were more people in the Holiday Inn than ever before. The management had covered the Olympic size indoor swimming pool with flooring, and then put seats wherever they found space.

As Clark and Shelly looked from behind the stage curtain, Clark told Shelly. "This is the most people we have played to, and I sure hope they like what we do."

Fifteen minutes into the concert, he had his answer. The crowd was his, and he sang his heart out. They loved it. Shelly had chills run up and down her spine.

She loved Clark, but had never seen him turned loose on a set down audience before. Up till now Two Plus One Country had played mostly dances and occasionally a small club concert. This was different. These people had paid for their seat. Near the end he ran out of songs he wrote, so he resorted to cover songs. It made no difference to the crowd. They loved Clark, and didn't give a phiss what he sang. The manager had called on the local police for crowd control. It was a good thing, because when the curtain closed the crowd came to its feet and about a hundred crazed fans charged the band stand, while the rest gave Clark his first standing ovation since grade school. The applause was sustained, as Clark took another bow.

People were being restrained from jumping on the stage by the cops. Clark knew, from now on he had to think about security; after all the word fan had been watered down from fanatic, and if you had fans then you needed protection from them.

The two week furlough came to an end too soon for everyone. Shelly wanted to go back to Rucker with Clark, but she was only a week from reporting for her junior year at university, and couldn't possibly make it. Clark came close to asking her to marry him, but knew it would be the end of her education. He told her he would marry her when she graduated with a degree, if she still wanted him. She hugged him and said. "Thank you sweetheart, for being stronger than me. If it was my choice, we would see a preacher today, and I'll never change my mind, I am yours for better or worse, forever."

YOU'RE MOVING WHERE?

Back at Fort Rucker, Doc and Clark were assigned lodging in a World War Two wood barracks with thirty beds in a dorm like affair. Each man had a wall locker, foot locker, and a metal bunk. They had to carry all this stuff from the company supply room to their assigned area.

There was a Corporal in charge of Clark and Doc's barracks. He was a pretty nasty sort, and liked to give the young recruits a hard time. He finally got around to Clark. He was shorter then Clark by a foot and seem to find pleasure in confronting a taller man. He stuck his face nose to nose in Doc's face, and gave him a hard time about his messy area. Then he tried to do the same to Clark, but Clark stood up as tall as he could and looked over the little corporal's head. After the corporal ran down and lapsed into silence, Clark couldn't hold his laughter any longer and began shaking with mirth. The little man screamed at Clark and Clark only laughed harder. The rest of the troops began to laugh at the impossible little man. He finally ran out of the barracks. Clark felt sorry for the guy and went in search of him. He found the young man right outside the door. He apologized to the Corporal. The little man was almost in tears. He asked, "Why did you laugh at me?"

Clark said, "You reminded me of another corporal from another time is all. Don't treat us bad and we won't laugh at you."

He left the man standing there wondering what corporal he was talking about. Throughout the eight week course the little corporal would seek Clark out to talk to him about things. Clark found him to be a nice person who had only misconstrued how a corporal treated those under him.

The two musicians excelled in the aircraft maintenance course. Clark found some of the course boring, and had to work hard to keep him and Doc awake. The one class they both enjoyed was with an instructor by the name SSGT Delbert Q Rivers. No one slept through one of his classes. He was dynamic and entertaining, and always moving all over the classroom. The forty students had to follow him with their eyes for the entire fifty minute class. They had SGT Rivers for one class a day for the eight week course.

The class began normally. Sgt Rivers was in good form. His uniform was meticulous like always and he was teaching them fuel systems for fixed winged aircraft. In particular, the U1A Otter, when the jolly green giant, a Mr. Green, came in the classroom and took a seat at the rear. He was the civilian fixed wing evaluator for instructors. He would evaluate SSgt Rivers on presentation and material. The class room door opened and a two star general, a one star general, and more colonels then Clark thought possible, entered the class room and stood at the rear.

Rivers seemed to come more alive. He absolutely bristled with know-how, and delivered the best class the commanding general and Mr. Green had ever witnessed. Everyone felt like clapping, but that's not done in a military school. Clark heard later that Sgt Rivers had been nominated for instructor of the year by both Mr. Green's report, and the commanding general's recommendation. As far as Clark and Doc were concerned Rivers was the best instructor in the entire us Army. They learned more about maintaining aircraft from him, than all the rest combined.

The last week of the course was slow for the two musicians. With three days remaining, they were called in to see the company commander. The two reported all proper like and the Captain stood and shook their hand. His name tag read Watkins. He had known for some time he had a celebrity in his company, but he didn't want to interfere with his training. He told them to take a seat, and then asked, "Do you boys know a Brad Johns?"

Clark said. "We sure do, he's played lead guitar with us for years. Why do you ask sir?"

Capt. Watkins smiled and said. "Because, he is standing right behind you."

Pandemonium, instantly took place. The three were slapping each on the back, and embracing one another. The Commanding officer loved country music and stood there with a big grin on his face. After they settled down, he said, "You boys aren't going back to an aviation unit when you leave here; you're being assigned to Brads unit, a Special Service Company on post. The commanding officer, a Colonel Frank, called me a few weeks back and arranged it all through Department of the Army. As soon as I release you, you go straight to his unit. You don't even have to clear post."

The three old friends had some catching up to do, and the Captain told them they had the rest of the day off. The graduating ceremonies were tomorrow and then they could sign out of his unit, then go and sign in to their new unit. He said. "Now you three get on out of here and enjoy yourselves."

CHAPTER 5
LIFE IN THE ARMY

Life for the three soldiers settled down to a semi boring routine that consisted of playing music or practicing it. They had excellent private rooms, in a new block building and the chow wasn't too bad either. The three played wherever the Army wanted them to. Their first job was opening at the NCO club for Ernest Tubb. ET told Clark. "I sure like the way you deliver a song." He suggested Clark bring his outfit to Nashville and look him up. He would help him anyway he could. Clark thanked Ernest; explaining he belonged to the US Army for the next two and half years, after that he would see.

They played all over the middle south, at different bases. There were some chances for Clark to meet with Shelly and he did. She came down on Easter Break and spent an entire week with him, then went home to her grandmother for a week. She called him every day at the insistence of Ellie.

Clark talked to Ellie and asked how she was, all Ellie would say was; she was getting old you know, and then laughed. Clark thought she was a neat person and never missed a chance to see her.

Clark and the boys had just returned from Ft Benning Georgia, when the charge of quarters came to Clark's room and handed him a note. It read call Shelly. URGENT. Clark ran to the pay phone at the company headquarters and called Shelly, whom he had just left two hours before. She picked up on the first ring, and said, Clark? He said yes honey what is it. Shelly was crying as she said Ellie's had a heart attack and is in the ICU at Macon Hospital. I'm leaving now, do you think you can come too."

Clark told her. "You know I will, I'll arrange for an emergency leave right away."

The charge of quarters had overheard and was already on the phone to Col Frank. He received verbal orders for Clark to proceed on a ten day leave starting now. Clark signed out in the company book and ran to tell the other boys he had to go, now. The other boys would come down on a two weeks leave starting tomorrow. After all; there was nothing they could do without Clark to do the singing.

When Clark reached Macon, he drove straight to the hospital. Shelly was in the waiting room at the ICU. She came in his arms when she saw him. He asked Shelly, how is Ellie doing? Shelly though tears said, "The doctor said he would talk to us when you arrived."

Shelly was really upset about her grandmother and Clark was concerned as well. Ellie was going on eighty-six and was bucking the odds on longevity. Clark thought, if she died, Shelly would be all alone in the world except for him and he was stuck off in the Army.

On sudden Impulse he got down on his Knee and took Shelly's hands in his. He asked, Shelly will you marry me? Shelly stopped weeping and grabbed him in a hard hug, saying, "Yes, yes, I'll be your wife. Oh Gran will be so happy. I am so happy, I love you Clark."

He said, "I love you and it doesn't matter if you have a degree or not, my music career is on the right track and you belong by my side. I've heard you sing now for a while, and I tell you, all you need is some exposure, and you will get that with me, but not stuck off in some office somewhere." Shelly had never looked at it in that light before and was thrilled down to her toes.

The Doctor came in the room and led them to an office off to the side. He told them Ellie was stable and in no pain. She did need an operation, however. A pacemaker must be installed in her chest. This would regulate her heart rate and she should resume normal life after that. The news made the newly engaged couple happy. They went home and had a wonderful night. Ellie had her operation the following day and it was a success. She would be staying in the hospital for six more days to make sure there were no complications, and then be coming home.

Clark and Shelly went around town to see their many friends. Everyone they met was happy for them. Ruby and Diller had sold the house and Clark felt a sense of loss when he and Shelly drove by the place. Ruby and Diller had moved to Florida and he called them a couple times a month.

They were driving down Dennis drive when someone began honking their horn at the two. Clark pulled into the Quick Trip, and a brand new ford mustang pulled up beside them. Clark and Shelly almost fell out of his truck. It was Brad and Doc in the car. Doc said, "Thought you could get away from us did you?"

They all had a laugh at that. Clark asked Brad where he got the car, Brad said, "I have an Uncle who owns a dealership and guaranteed I could get financed. Now all I have to do is pay for it, Doc said he will help if I get in trouble."

The mustang was a new sixty-seven model and was fire engine red with black interior.

YOU'RE MOVING WHERE?

"Sharp", was all Clark and Shelly could think of to say. When Clark told them about him and Shelly's engagement, the two guys let out a rebel yell that was heard by someone who called the cops, and told them a fight was going on in the QT parking lot. Delmas Quead was the cop on duty and came screaming into the lot with lights going. He slid to a stop, jumped out and said, "What the hell is going on here?"

All three boys had attended school with Delmas and they had all been friends. Clark said, "Just what the hell do you think is going on here Delmas?"

Delmas recognized the three then and, his face turned crimson red and he said "Aw hell it's you guys, some dumb ass said a big fight was happening down here. How have you guys been?"

He went around and shook hands with all of them. Clark introduced Shelly to him and just before Delmas made an ass of himself, by making a play for Shelly. He said. "Shelly and I are engaged as of last night." Delmas got redder in the face and declared he had important work to do elsewhere, he then jumped in his car and tore out of the parking lot. All four of the bunch just about cracked up laughing after he left.

CHAPTER 6
THE TV SHOW

The phone rang and the guy introduced himself as Rick Moseman from TV four MCAN. He said, "We are interested in producing a live show with you and your band. It'll show each Saturday afternoon. Are you interested?"

Clark was excited. A live show would sure improve their popularity considerably. Clark asked Rick if he knew he and the band played music for the Army at the present and wasn't always available for local gigs. Rick said, "I didn't know that, maybe we had better wait until you get out.

Clark said. "We could do a few on tapes and you can show them at a later date".

Rick become excited and said. "Man what a great Idea. Come on down and sign a contract and let's get started."

Clark called his other players and told them the news. They thought it was a good thing as well.

YOU'RE MOVING WHERE?

The Fargo bunch got off to a slow start on the first show because the recording engineer stopped Clark in mid song and wanted to redo it the way he wanted to hear it. Finally Clark put down his Bass and walked to the control booth, entered and closed the door. He told the guy to turn the microphone off to the studio.

All the boys saw through the window was Clark's back, but they knew Clark was doing all the talking, When recording resumed, no more interruptions took place, and it was "yes sir" and "no sir" from the man in the booth.

The boys had to learn a lot in a short time. The lights were hard on them. They had to let the makeup artist do them up every time the cameras were turned off. Mostly after the initial setting, they were only touched up.

Rick was pleasantly surprised at how good the band looked on camera. Clark learned to play to the camera before five minutes had passed. He had watched the live news cast and saw the red and green eye and correctly assumed red was shut up, and green was you better be saying something buddy, dead time on television was a no no in the industry.

That week they recorded a total of seven shows. Rick was tickled pink. He had been right, this boy Clark, would be a star someday. He paid Clark one thousand per show. Clark gave each musician two grand and Doc said "Holy double D man, that's good money!"

Clark took his three thousand and out of it he bought two gold rings for his wedding.

The leave ended too soon for the entire band. Ellie came home from the hospital a new woman. Before her heart attack, she had always been tired all the time, but now, she had energy to spare. Within two days of getting home, she began cooking up a storm. She made Clark bring Doc and Brad over and she fed them silly. They all laughed and kidded Ellie that she needed to go to the hospital more often.

Clark had to drive back early because he had only taken ten days leave. He told Shelly he would return in a month and they would get married. Shelly told him, "If you think for a second, you're going back to Fort Rucker without me; you have lost your mind Clark Fargo!"

Clark knew she was right, so they packed the truck up with things to set house keeping up in some rented whatever, and Shelly's education ended, at least for the moment.

Clark took Shelly in and introduced her to his commanding officer, Stanly Frank. The colonel was taken by Shelly and told Clark he was a lucky man. He also offered to help the two anyway he could. Clark said, "Well sir, I need time off to find someplace for us to live."

YOU'RE MOVING WHERE?

The Colonel said, "Take all the time you need. Just keep us posted on where you are."

Clark, Doc and Brad had all been promoted to Specialist fourth class while on leave. This upped their pay considerably. Clark and Shelly went out to Daleville Alabama. There were lots of mobile home parks there that rented to GIs from Rucker. They drove from park to park, and all were full up. They were told at the last one, there was a new one being built on the road opposite the Cairns field gate, down near the end of the road. The two drove down the sandy dirt road till a sign in red letters read Rivers Mobile Home Park. Clark pulled through the park and followed the office sign to the rear of a large new house. The place was as neat as anything they had seen at all the other parks. For some reason Clark got good vibes from this place. When he knocked on the back door and it opened, he damn near fainted! Standing there smiling at him was his favorite Instructor, SSGT Rivers. Rivers remembered Clark. He said, "Hello Fargo, what can I do for you?"

Clark said, "I saw the name of the park, but I didn't put it all together until now. Do you own this park?"

Del answered in the affirmative.

Del told him he didn't intend to spend all his life in the Army and he was building this place to take care of his finances after the Army. He wanted to know all about Clark. Consequently the two were becoming friends.

Del played a bit of guitar. But he admitted to Clark he wasn't much more than a wanta be guitar picker, but he could hold his own as a singer, in fact, he told Clark and Shelly about the time he hitchhiked all the way out to California, when he couldn't take his step father's harsh treatment for another second.

He had cousins in Porterville, in central California, and he lit amongst them and tried his hand at picking oranges with his cousin Reba Kiker. Del said, "I picked fruit when I was very young, but not oranges."

Reba clued him in on how it was done, and in a short time he was out picking her. He would set the ladder and literally run up the thing to the top, and while singing at the top of his lungs, cut fruit down to the ground once again. He'd dump his bag in boxes and repeated the process.

The year was 1966 and Hank Williams was still hot on the music charts, although he had expired on the rear seat of his caddy a year past on New Year's Day. Del loved Hank songs and sang them in his own style at the top of his considerable range. He particular loved "Your Cheating Heart", and after singing it on top of his

YOU'RE MOVING WHERE?

24 foot, three legged ladder, He heard applause at the bottom of the ladder.

When he looked down, every Okie and Mexican in the field was gathered there and right in the center of them was the straw boss. He wasn't clapping. He had a stern look on his face and crooked his finger at Del, indicating he should come down. When he arrived at the bottom he attempted to reset his ladder as he always did. The straw boss said, "Don't reset, you won't need it. I can't have you up there, my pickers aren't picking the fruit, they're too busy listening to you sing."

He handed Del his pay and said, "I put an extra twenty in there, now let me tell you, you are a fine singer and need to go find a place to sing so you don't keep other folk from their work."

He was smiling the entire time. Del said, "My cousin Reba was a little banty rooster of a human being, and she wanted to kick the crap out of that straw boss."

Del told her, that maybe he had been paid a very high complement by that straw boss, and had done the only thing he could do to get his pickers to pick. Del told Clark and Shelly all he did was go join the Army, and here they were.

He asks if he could help them in anyway. Clark said, "I will be stationed here until I complete my enlistment and we need a place to live, do you have anything for rent?"

Del ask them how long would they stay. Clark said, "If it's a nice place, until my discharge." Del said, "I'll buy a brand new 12x50 for you two and put it on the lot of your choice."

Clark and Shelly become excited. "How much will the rent be?" Shelly asked.

Del said, "My payment on it should be $125 per month. Can you afford $225 a month? You'll have electricity on top of that." Del said.

Shelly said. "Yes we can afford that."

Clark said, "The lady has spoken. When can we move in?"

Del said, "I'll make the call and they will bring it right out, and if they can't I'll tow it with my truck. You two can move in tomorrow night."

Do you have a place to stay tonight? Del asked. Clark said, "We will stay at a motel tonight."

Del said, "That's good, you saved my three daughters from sleeping all in one bed."

As Clark and Shelly headed to the motel, Shelly, commented; "I really like Sgt Rivers."

Clark said, "I do too honey, and I'm real happy he is making us a place to live."

Shelly said, "Let's go get Brad and Doc and go out and eat somewhere to celebrate."

Clark said, "We are on the way, butter cup."

YOU'RE MOVING WHERE?

When the two arrived at their company, they found Brad and Doc in the dayroom playing pool. The two perked up, and readily accepted Clark and Shelly's invitation. Brad said, "Yeah, we were not even, looking forward to Mess hall food."

Brad said, "Let's go in my Mustang, you can leave your truck at the motel and ride to the Strip with us." The strip he referred to was just across the Dale county line.

There were beer joints and restaurants all along a five mile section of the highway. The return through a dry county was known as DWI alley, and many a stripe had been lost to prove it.

The restaurant the Fargo bunch made their way to was a nice place that looked at first, like, nothing but a rather large colonel house. When they entered it was everything but a house. The restaurant was one of the poshest Clark had ever been in. If the food was prepared on the same level, they were in for a treat. They weren't disappointed whatsoever.

When the Bunch had eaten their fill, they were completely satisfied; they had picked the best eating place in the area. The only thing Clark saw was, they needed a small combo playing mood music to make it more perfect

CHAPTER 7
MARRIED LIFE

The wedding was the biggest event to take place in Macon Georgia in years. Clark was the first celebrity to have an open wedding where the public was invited, ever! Ellie thought it might be a mistake, but she went along, as Clark did with her only granddaughter's wishes and nuptials. A huge red, white, and blue tent had been rented and erected on the front lawn of her house.

Catering was acquired for a hundred people. Little did they know, four times that many would show up, all of them hungry. Clark saved the day by spending more money than he had. He bought all the Kentucky Fried Chicken the local store could produce in a four hour period. This made the Macon Subscriber front page, the headline read; COUNTRY SINGER BUY'S KENTUCKY FRIED CHICKEN BUSINESS FOR A DAY, TO CATER HIS AND HIS BRIDE'S WEDDING. The story went on to tell why so many guest showed up uninvited. Seems The

YOU'RE MOVING WHERE?

Fargo bunch had mentioned Clark's wedding date on air, during the television show they did live two days before the wedding. The singer's popularity assured a crowd, and Clark Fargo had done well for them. As someone said, "Have you ever seen so many chicken bones in your life?"

The wedding was talked about for years, and was referred to as the Great Fargo Chicken Munch. There was a dump truck full of bones that went to the dump. Clark and Two Plus One Country band would be long remembered in Macon by Clark's generosity.

Clark was worried about how he and Shelly were going to pay for all this generosity on an E-5's pay. The boys had all been promoted to specialist fifth class recently. While it meant more money at the pay table, it wouldn't help pay for all that chicken that a good portion of Macon had consumed at his expense. Ellie came to their rescue. She knew they didn't have enough money to meet the bill, so she called her bank and told them to pay Kentucky Fried Chicken for the chicken and to add ten percent on top, for their trouble. Clark was so grateful he hugged and thanked her. Shelly had tears in her eyes. She said, "Thank you Gran, I don't know what we would do if you weren't here to help us."

Ellie said, "Your grandfather left me with a goodly amount of money and it has been invested in cash deposits. Over the years it has grown considerable, and I can't take it with me. There's no baggage compartment in a hearse. I want you two to go down and pick out a nice motor home. It will be your wedding present, and; I had my banker to start a bank account in your name at me bank and deposit 10,000 dollars in it for the two of you. Now, no more thanks are necessary. You go and find that motor home and call me, and I'll call the bank and fix it all up." They both hugged Elli.

The honeymoon was fun in the new motor home. They hit Alabama, Tennessee and parts of Georgia they didn't know existed. Then they drove to Fort Rucker and then to their home at Rivers Mobil Home court. They loved the twelve by fifty mobile home. He had kept his word and purchased the unit for them on their word that they would rent it for a long spell.

Clark and Shelly had become good friends with Del Rivers and his family. Del had three girls and one son. They were polite and well mannered children. Del's wife was German and seemed nice as well. Del told Clark he was on orders to go to Vietnam in June of next year. He wasn't looking forward to the ordeal, but he was a career solider and it was his job.

YOU'RE MOVING WHERE?

He asks Clark if he and the boys would play at his barbecue here in his park. Clark told him, "You bet Sgt Rivers, just tell me when."

Rivers shook Clark's hand and told him, "For starters, my name is Del and I want you to use it. We've known each other quite awhile now, and I think we can drop the rank OK?"

Clark said, "Sure Del. When do we play?"

"How about we make it my birthday, it comes on August the second. I'll turn twenty-seven then." Clark said, "Let me clear it with my CO and if he OK's it, you're on."

August the second turned up hot and clear. Del had built the stage under big hundred year old pines. The park had once been part of a cotton plantation before the turn of the century, and Del had purchased the land from the granddaughter of the original slave owner. Del had many friends and most of them showed up.

Del introduced a fellow by the name of Duke Fletcher to the bunch. Del said, "Duke is a good picker and I thought you might let him sit in today."

Clark liked Duke from the get go, and asks him what instruments he played. Duke said, "I play anything with strings on it, but I prefer fiddle."

Clark said, "Grab your fiddle and come on, we'll treat this as a practice session."

Theodore Potter

After one song, Clark knew they had struck gold in this fiddle player. Duke played all the songs Clark wrote, plus he never faltered once. Before the set ended, Two Plus One Country was transformed into three plus one country. The Fargo bunch grew by a quarter on that day. Del Rivers got up and sang some of the best songs of the day. He was immensely popular anyhow and if the concert were inside, he would have brought the house down. Clark told Del he was welcome to sing with the bunch at any future concerts also. Del explained to Clark he wanted to improve his guitar playing then maybe, he would play with them. If they liked his playing that is.

CHAPTER 8
TRIP TO VIETNAM

Clark read the bulletin board at the company every day. The board was the musicians contact with their first SGT and company commander Colonel Frank. There was a note for Clark to see Col Frank ASAP. Clark knocked on The Colonel's door and he was told to enter. Frank greeted him as an equal and invited him to set. He made small talk and then dropped his bomb. He said, "You and the boys are going to do a tour of Vietnam."

Clark's heart fell to the bottom of his chest and his whole life passed before his eyes in an instant. Frank said, "It's not as bad as you think it to be, you are meeting up with Robyn Gantry and her lead guitar picker, a Dunkyn Rollings. You guys will do nine shows in country then one in the Philippines, and one in Honolulu. your final concert will be at fort Ord, near Oakland, for the troops bound for Vietnam, and the first show you do will also be at Ord."

Clark said, "Sir I have two requests, one, a SSgt Duke Fletcher, over in rotary wing systems, is our fiddle player and we pretty much need him on this tour. The other thing is, if at all possible, we need Shelly with us. She keeps us all together and I would appreciate it very much if she could go with us."

Col Frank was silent for a moment then he said, "I'll do all I can to make it happen. The tour doesn't take off for another month. Let's see this is August, the tour starts on the twenty-eighth of September; we should be able to set it all up by then. Bring SSgt Fletcher by to see me, will you?"

When Clark broke the news to Shelly, she was both excited and apprehensive at the same time, "What if they won't let me go with you? I'll be stuck here without you."

Clark took her in his arms and said, "Trust Colonel Frank, he will do the right thing by us. He will fight long and hard until he gets what we want."

Little did they know what a battle Stan Frank had with the Department of Army. At first the General flatly said, "NO".

Stan Frank being a negotiator, countered with, "These two are a team, and this boy is a star, and I want to keep them together."

YOU'RE MOVING WHERE?

The General wasn't so adamant, but he still said, "Dependents aren't allowed in combat zones."

Colonel Frank said, "Robyn Gantry is taking her husband with her."

This finally got through to the General. He said, "OK. I'll go out on a limb and sign the orders. We both better pray she doesn't get her butt shot off over there, because if she does, you and I can hang up our bird and star, because our career's will be over."

Clark got Duke by the collar and drug him up to Stan Frank. Duke didn't much care for Colonels, but he liked Frank. He asked Duke where he had played before Fargo. Duke told how he had played all over Nashville and had even gone on the road with the Loretta Lynn show for a spell. Then the Army had drafted him, and at the end of his two years, he had re-upped for six years and here he was. Colonel Frank liked Duke. He asked, "How would you like to be a full time musician?"

Duke said, "Hey man that would be great. Can I stay with the Fargo's?"

Stan Frank said, "Yes, that's the reason I want you here in special services. I can put you with them full time."

Duke was happier than Clark had ever seen him. He said to Clark, "Man I want to thank you for getting me out of that instructional job, I was going nuts in there. What's on our agenda?"

Clark Grinned and said, "We're bound for Vietnam next month. Duke stopped in his tracks and turned to Clark and said, "Tell me I heard you wrong, before I go and shoot myself."

Clark was bent over laughing. He said, "We're doing nine shows with Robyn Gantry in country and some others in other countries too."

Duke said, "Man you scared the pee waddle out of me. Please don't' do that again."

Clark said, "OK man, welcome officially to the Fargo bunch. You're one of us now, glad to have you aboard."

Clark took Duke out to his mobile home and told Shelly she had been okayed for the tour. She hugged him and said, "That is the most wonderful news I've heard all day."

Clark told Shelly, "We have a brand new member of our band and he is Duke Fletcher."

Shelly ran to ran to Duke, hugged him and said, "Welcome to the band Duke."

Duke's face got red, and he lost his tongue. He thought Shelly was the most beautiful woman in the world. He hoped someday, he could find a girl like her.

Clark called Brad and Doc and told them to come out and they would have some dinner and discuss their game plan. Clark had a list of requirements they must fulfill before their shipping date.

The Army would issue each of them two sets of dress blues, to be worn at all concerts. There were shots and physicals to be taken. They must report to personnel for a records check and then over to finance to arrange for advance pay. They wouldn't be able to draw any pay while on tour. Each would draw twenty dollars a day called TDY pay, and this could be drawn on in advance. There was a list of do's and don'ts and they discussed them and decided they were only common sense things and necessary for the good of all.

Shelly cooked up spaghetti and meat balls. The bunch lit in to them like they were starved. It all disappeared in a flash, leaving a glazed look on Shelly's face but, she was a very happy woman.

CHAPTER 9
DODGING BULLETS

The big jet sat down on the runway at Oakland, California with a thump that scared Shelly half to death. She had never flown before and had been holding onto Clark for dear life for most of the four hours of the trip. The rest of the bunch must have had a button in their butts, because just as soon as they left the ground back in Columbus, they were sound asleep. Clark enjoyed the trip and did his best to keep Shelly's mind off the flight.

Now here they were on the bus to the terminal, and would meet the Gantry's momentarily. Clark saw Robyn and walked over and introduced himself and Shelly. Robyn and Shelly hit it off, right off the bat. Clark shook hands with Mr. Robyn Gantry, he said his name was Lofty, and Clark understood why, the guy was six foot seven at least. Lofty introduced Dunkyn Rollings, the guitar picker. Dunkyn was a nice shy sorta fellow. Clark liked him. He took him over to his Bunch, and intros were made.

The musicians went off to talk among themselves while Clark rejoined his wife and Robyn. Clark told her, "I sure like the way you sing Mrs. Gantry."

She said, "Here now, my name is Robyn, Can I call you Clark?"

The group had one practice session, and then played at the huge game arena in Oakland. Over 30,000 soldiers either coming from or going to Vietnam packed the place. Robyn had her song "I Don't Wanta Walk Alone". That was hot on the charts, at number twelve, and climbing fast. Her last hit, "You Cheated Me Right Out Of You" was still on the charts at number forty-one. The crowd was primed for Robyn Gantry.

The stage was all set up. The Fargo's were to open. They were in place, in their dress blue uniforms. When the curtain slowly opened from the center, all four musicians were standing at attention and saluting the 30.000 men in the audience. A great cheer arose from the fans. When it died down Clark sang one of his favorite songs written by Del Rivers, called "Fly Away Little Girl'. It had a falsetto part in the chores and the fans were dead quiet until the last note sounded. They stood and wouldn't stop clapping or sit down until Clark sang the last verse and a chorus again. Even then the applause was sustained.

Shelly told Clark that Robyn had remarked; "Damn, I must get one of those blue uniforms."

This almost cracked Shelly and Lofty up. Clark sang three more songs with much the same reception, and then, introduced Robyn Gantry. The fans raised the roof as she came on. Dunkyn Rollings and Brad Johns exchanged places. Dunkyn knew Robyn's material back to front. The show went off without a hitch. Robyn worked her special magic on the crowd for an hour and a half. The finale was, "Blues Train". The fans sang it with gusto, and then, the show was over. They all had to do three curtain calls. Clark had made 30,000 new fans. What a trip he thought.

The troop flew to Hawaii and played at Ford Barracks, at an outside concert. The base had been opened to the public. Don Ho agreed to appear, so this brought the locals out in force. The parade ground was filled with an estimated 50,000 bodies, and the night was a tremendous success.

Clark, the boys, and Shelly really liked Don Ho. He invited them to his Club as his guest, but they had to decline. The troop had to catch a plane to Manila, in the Philippines. Clark told him

YOU'RE MOVING WHERE?

they would make it a point on their return trip. Don grinned, and shook all their hands. He would be happy to accommodate the bunch on their return.

Shelly was getting used to flying now, and wanted to set in a window every time they boarded a flight. The rest of the Bunch simply slept the entire trip except mealtime. None of them ever drank alcohol except Duke, and he gave it up for the sake of them all. So there was nothing else to do, except eat and sleep. Shelly Said, "They all do it so well." Robyn and Lofty laughed and agreed with her

Manila was a repeat of Ford barracks. The show was so tight by now it went by so quick it seemed to Brad, he wasn't doing much at all. He sure wished he could do more on the show. Out of boredom he asked Duke if he could borrow his Mandolin to learn to play. Duke said, "Sure I'll even show you a few chords, if you like."

Brad spent every spare moment plunking on the little instrument. By the fourth show in country he was on stage playing

The group of entertainers went first to Saigon and then were flown out by helicopters to the different bases, to do their shows. There was super tight security and a few times, trips were cancelled without any reason. Duke was on his second trip over here, and explained, "If in-tell came in that enemy action might cause harm to the group, the show was called off."

The last show was at the Vietnam Rest and Recreation center, Vung Tau, down on the coast of South Vietnam. There were a lot of aviation companies permanently stationed there plus an average of 10,000 in-country men there at any given time, resting up from the war. About half of them were Vietnamese soldiers, and wouldn't give a damn about country music anyhow. As the boys were setting up the tons of gear, a Sergeant walked up to them. He just stood there, until Clark looked up and said, "Yes Sarge what can I do for you?"

Clark then let out a yell that startled the others and made some look for cover. Clark said, "Hey guys look, if it ain't our friend Del Rivers!"

Things were a bit crazy as the band, Brad, Doc and Duke charged and pummeled the heck out of Del. They knew he was over here, and hoped they'd see him before they went home.

Clark ask Del what he was doing down here. Del pointed at a revetment containing one large single engine otter aircraft, and said, "Keeping seventeen of those crates in the air. They call us the Teeny Weenie Airlines, you call, we haul, you all."

YOU'RE MOVING WHERE?

The boys laughed their butts off at that. Clark said, "I want you to sing with my set tonight OK"?

Del said, "Sure, I've got my guitar picking straightened out and I'll bring it too.

The show had a slight deviation that night. Del Rivers, SSgt - Career soldier; sang and played to the very men he had to tell what to do each day. At first the GI's didn't react in a positive way to Del, until his third song when he sang Bobby Bares' "I Wanta Go Home."

The fiddle work Duke put in that song brought tears to many a lonely soldier's eyes, on this far-side of the earth. When the song ended the crowd went wild and came to its feet. As Del walked off stage, the fans began to chant, we want Del. We want Del. They began to stamp their right foot in time to the chant. The thousands of GI jungle boots sounded like nothing anyone had ever heard before. Clark looked at Robyn, and she motioned for him to bring Del back on. Del had turned around, and was looking at Clark, when Clark said in the mic; "Do you want Del back out here?"

The fans drowned him out, before he could get it all said. Del came to the microphone and stood there in silence. When it became silent Del said, "Do you wonderful friends of mine, and all these wonderful folks know what you have

Theodore Potter

done? You've made me realize, I am in the wrong line of work, I need to go ahead and become a full time singer."

Someone in the audience, stood up and said, in a thundering voice, "That's right, now shut up and sing, Please."

The GI's went wild once more. Del turned to the Fargo's and said, "Let's do a medley of Hag songs. Follow my lead and break after every song, then pick up on the new beat."

Del did :The Bottle Let Me Down" in "C", "Sing Me Back Home" in "G", "Branded Man" in "D", and topped them off, with his complete version of "Okie From Muskogee" in "E". The crowd was once more on its feet when Del walked off stage. Clark looked at Robyn and shrugged his shoulders as an apology. Robyn said as she passed Clark, "Its ok hon. It gives me something to work to. Maybe I should be the Sergeant."

She was smiling and came on and did the best show of her career. The crowd was whipped into a frenzy. By the time Robyn finished her show, they were on their feet screaming. She had to come out and do some more of her current hits. Finally it was over, and the band was all wrung out.

Clark only realized now, he was wringing wet with sweat. He glanced at the rest of the band,

YOU'RE MOVING WHERE?

and saw they all had the same wilted look about them. They all laughed, while looking at each other. Doc said, "Man what a show!"

The others nodded agreement.

CHAPTER 10
BACK HOME

Don Ho was a man of his word. When the bunch landed in Honolulu the show was granted time off to rest up. They were given Quarters at Ford Barracks in the officers BOQ. It didn't seem to matter to the transportation and housing officer that the highest rank among them was Duke, as a SSG E-6. They had a civilian with them and by damn he had seen the show, and loved it. He had plenty of room and that was that.

After resting for a day, the entire bunch invaded Don Ho's club. He welcomed them with open arms. He was a massive fellow and made two of Clark. He gathered the whole bunch in a bear hug. He said, "My club is your club and your money is no good in here, my staff will alert me if you try to pay."

He laughed long and loud at his own joke. Clark said, "Only if you let us get up and sing a few songs".

YOU'RE MOVING WHERE?

Don said, "Well, I was gonna ask you anyway." They had a fun evening, and were invited to come and sing anytime they were in town.

CHAPTER 11

June of 1969 found the Fargo bunch playing gig after gig for the Army. Doc, Brad and Clark were promoted to S/SGT E-6 in June of 1969. S/Sgt Rivers returned to Ft Rucker and resumed teaching. They had one heck of a reunion when he arrived home.

Del was more distant than before for some reason, probably because of all he had seen in Vietnam. A man can't see men die for a year and not have it to affect him in some way. He had watched his best friend Ken Hughes, die in a senseless crash at Ben Hue air base. An Air Force plane, simply clipped his wing off, in a maneuver, later forbidden by the Air Force. All this, Del carried on his shoulders without sharing it with anyone.

Clark heard Del had come back to a wife who had cheated on him with others since the day he left for Vietnam. He found this out while he was still in Vietnam. A weaker man would have come unglued, but Del's moral fiber was

YOU'RE MOVING WHERE?

woven tighter than most men. He thought of his kids whom he worshipped, and tucked his chin in and decided to remove his cheating wife down under to Australia.

Del and Clark were closer now and talked a great deal. Del said, "Clark this music business here in the USA is being controlled by a few men such as Ernest Tubb, Roy Acuff and a hand full of major record labels, mostly in Nashville. In order to crack the nut you must know someone as close as you and I know each other. I can't see that as a possibility for me. You know some big names in the business and you need to make the most of it. The US Army got in your way and now it's in mine. I will get out, come the thirtieth of October. I'll sell out and move to Australia, where they don't even know what country music is, and, then make my bid for fame."

Clark was amazed at how articulate Del was, describing the situation. He and Shelly, along with all the Fargo Band would miss the fire out of Del Rivers.

CHAPTER 12

In the first week of December Colonel Frank called and asked Clark and Shelly to come out to his house for dinner. Frank lived in a nice ranch style house in Ozark, Alabama. When they arrived they found Mrs. Frank to be a most gracious hostess, and Col Frank was right there with her. Col Frank said, "We will dispense with rank calling, my name is Stan from now on, and this is my wife of twenty-on years Nora. Honey this is the nicest couple; I ever had the privilege to know, Clark and his lovely wife Shelly."

Nora said, "Oh, it's so wonderful to meet you at last. Stan tells me so many wonderful things about you, I feel like I'm meeting royalty."

The dinner was superb, and the conversation intelligent and stimulating. Clark and Shelly enjoyed it so much they almost didn't catch Stan's statement. Clark said, "Hey what did you say sir."

Stan laughed and repeated it. He said, "You and your band can get an early out with only one exception. That being Duke. He drew a re-enlistment bonus and must serve all his time. There is a slight hang up with you three boys."

Clark and Shelly held their breath, while Stan Frank composed his next words. He said, "MACV was much impressed with you and your band on the Gantry tour. They want you to headline your own tour. I told them only if you get credit for a full tour in Vietnam and an early out. They pretty much agreed with everything except one. Shelly can't go. The places you will play, just aren't secure enough. You will only be in country for ten days, and do ten shows, then back here and be discharged from the service."

Clark looked at Shelly and asked, "Do you think you can handle that babe?"

Shelly, with brightness she didn't feel, said, "I'll go home and be with Gran, until you come back."

There was a damper on the rest of the evening, as Clark and Shelly said Goodnight, Stan said, "We really enjoyed your company, we'll do it again someday."

Clark and Shelly drove in silence for a bit, then Shelly asks Clark, "Just how much danger will you guys be in over there?"

Clark said, "Nothing is guaranteed in a war zone, but I'm sure all precautionary measures will be taken, don't you think?"

Theodore Potter

Shelly agreed and they brightened up and enjoyed themselves.

YOU'RE MOVING WHERE?

CHAPTER 13

Clark said out loud, "Damn those 122 mm rockets anyhow. I'm sure glad Shelly's not along on this trip."

This was the second time tonight they and their four man MP security detail, had dove into this bunker. The 122's were horrendous and sprayed little pieces of metal in a thousand directions. The boys could hear the metal hit the sand bags that covered them with a foot of protection. Doc Said, "Hell, next time I'm bringing my bed in here and get some sleep!"

It was a much needed light moment and they all laughed. The attack was over in minutes and they filed back into their quarters. They had one more show to do before leaving Vietnam forever. Come morning a helicopter would deliver them back to MACV headquarter, for their final show. All nine shows had been a resounding success. Clark and his band had made many fans over here. These men came from all walks of life and every part of the USA and the world. They were hungry for a taste of home. But at the same time, if The Band was a bad one, they would have been booed off the stage.

The flight from Vietnam stopped off in Sydney Australia and it brought R&R troops from Vietnam. It was the only flight out that had room for the band and all their gear. Clark talked the Army into allowing them to lay over three days in Sydney, for a little R&R for the band. The 2 single boys all hit the hotel bars up at Kings Cross, and soon had a pretty Australian lass on their arms. There were two girls to each male in the huge city of six million, so they were told. Clark spent the three days exploring. The new Opera house the Aussies were in the process of building intrigued Clark. It seemed to be on an Island in the middle of the bay. He took photos of it to show Shelly and Ellie on his return.

The boys brought their dates to the rooms they had taken at the Wentworth and introduced them to Clark. All three girls were cute as can be, and were thrilled to meet a real live country music star from America. They saw Clark's wedding ring and it cooled their ardor somewhat. They still wanted to hang near Clark, so he faked a yawn, and said he had to get some sleep. The three guys smiled at Clark and winked their thanks. The three went off to do whatever healthy girls and boys do when they meet in

YOU'RE MOVING WHERE?

another country. All Clark could think about was Shelly; he was tired of this hotel room and wished she was here.

He picked up the telephone and booked a call to Shelly. The operator said more sweetly than normal. I'll call you when the call comes through Mr. Fargo. There was syrup dripping from her words. Clark held the phone out and looked at in consternation. This was no country for a married man, he thought; with or without his wife by his side. Shelly came on the line and was so excited he couldn't get a word in sideways, she finally settled down when Clark reminded her, this call was costing them twelve dollars a minute. He told her he would be home in three days. Shelly said, "I'll come home so we can pack up and move, I love you and miss you like sin."

Clark said, "I miss you too honey, see you in three days."

CHAPTER 14

The huge 747 Boeing jet liner they left Sydney on, was a beautiful machine as far the band was concerned. Hell, Brad and Doc reckoned you could remove all the seats and play a game of football complete with by standers along the sides. The thing was so fuel efficient and with the west to east flow of the jet stream, they flew non-stop to LA in thirteen hours. What a trip, Duke had fallen off the wagon while with his Aussie girlfriend and damn near drank all the scotch up the plane had in store. Clark watched with affection, and realized there wasn't a mean bone in Duke's body, drunk or sober.

Duke finally had enough booze and stretched out on the seats and slept for eight full hours. If he was hung over, the rest of the bunch couldn't tell. However when ask by a flight attendant if he would care for a drink. Duke turned a bit green and vehemently shook his head no.

YOU'RE MOVING WHERE?

This tickled the other three non-drinkers. And Duke looked embarrassed by the whole thing. Clark thought he might crawl back on the wagon, and he was right. Clark figured Duke had a big heart and having no one at home, had brought on the bout with all those little bottles.

They had left Brad's Mustang and Clark's motorhome in long term parking in Dothan, Alabama. When they landed, the ton of gear was wheeled out to the motorhome, and loaded up. Twenty-six miles later they were back at Rucker. Shelly met Clark at the door of the mobile home and wrapped her legs around him. They didn't waste any time, they went to bed, and made love. To Clark's mind it had never been better or sweeter. Maybe a few days away from each other, was a good thing now and then.

CHAPTER 15

Not being in the Army any longer felt strange to the three original Two Plus One Country musicians. Duke had to stay behind. He still had two and half months to go. Clark thought Duke was going to cry when they parted company. Clark had a promise from Stan Frank that he would give Duke as much lee way as he could. Stan said, "I'll sign so many three day passes it may set some sort of record."

The two laughed at that. Duke would spend three days in Macon and four at Rucker. He also had thirty-four days accrued leave and would take them. That didn't leave too many days before the band's integrity would be restored to completeness.

Clark and Shelly moved back into the apartment above the garage. It sure was good to be home. Ellie had aged a lot in the three years since Clark left for the Army, and was frailer than ever. She was bright eyed and happy to see her two kids. She said, "I must talk to the two of you. I want to do it now, if that's OK with you."

They set down at the kitchen table; Ellie asked Shelly if she would serve coffee. Ellie looked like she was favoring her right side and it worried Clark. He asked her if she was OK. She gazed at this boy she had learned to love, and said, "We all get old, and I've had a good life and don't want to leave without taking care of loose ends."

She got up and walked to the writing desk and picked up a stack of papers. She sat down once more and seemed a bit out of breath. Shelly came in and poured coffee; Ellie held her hand up, saying, "None for me thanks. "

Ellie said, "You two are a perfect pair of grandchildren. I love you both so much. I should have done what I'm about to do a long time ago. I think, we think in our minds that we will never grow old and die. More and more I realize it will happen no matter what. I am naming the both of you as my executors. The funds in the bank and all cash deposit certificates have your names on them. The only funds remaining are my Social security checks and they stop, when I pass on, but they are enough to sustain me. My needs are few. Do you have any questions?"

The two were overcome and didn't know what to say, they just hugged the old lady. She said, "I'm a bit tired, I think I'll lay down for a bit. You can read these papers; they will tell you all you need to know."

Clark began to read the papers, they were from a lawyer's office, and were signed and had a raised seal affixed over Ellie's signature. One of them was a financial report. Checking: $41,034.21. Clark was shaking by now. Cash Deposits: $1,679,432.46. Clark almost fainted he couldn't look any more. All he knew was, he and his wife were rich beyond their wildest dreams. He looked at Shelly, she said, "I already knew about it. Gran was going to give it all to me and I told her I wouldn't take it if you weren't on it too, and she told me she had hoped I would feel that way. This house is to be ours, with the twelve acres of land. Of course there will be probate taxes to pay."

Clark was finding it a bit hard to breath, he just held his beautiful wife in his arm, as she held him. It was almost like a dream to Clark, as he remembered the day he came here.

CHAPTER 16

Clark and his band fell back in to music as civilians with more ease, than they thought they would. Clark signed a new agreement with Television Four MACN. They would receive fifteen hundred dollars for each show and forty percent of all endorsements from sponsors. Kentucky Fried Chicken jumped at the opportunity of becoming Fargo's full time sponsor. Clark shared the seven hundred dollar weekly check with his band.

Rick Mosman called Clark and said, "I need to come and sit down and talk to you face to face if that's OK with you Clark."

Clark said, "Why don't you come over and have dinner with Shelly and me?"

Rick asked, "Can I bring my wife, Jess?"

Clark said, "You bet, tomorrow ok?"

After the meal, Rick said, "Clark you are star quality, and I think I can help get you there, if that's what you want."

Clark was silent for a moment, and then said, "I don't need the money, but then, I never sing just for money, anyhow. I feel I have an obligation to my fans, to go as far as possible and I guess I must say I want it. Being a star is, however, not a priority in my life. I must think about the band, most of them have been with me since the beginning, and they make a living from music. It wouldn't be fair to see them having to struggle with some other singer. So, if you think you can help us, fire away."

Rick said, "I am good friends with Chet Atkins in Nashville. He is starting to produce recordings for RCA, and I mentioned your name to him, and told him about our little TV show down here. He sounded interested and told me to send him a recording on eight track and he would give it a listen. I'll go ahead and do that. We'll run one off of last week's show and I'll edit out all but the songs. Then all we can do is hope."

The boys in the band were thrilled that their music was to be heard by the great guitar picker, Chet Atkins. If Chet liked what he heard, it was Nashville for sure. Shelly only had one reservation. Her Gran was growing frailer each day. If Clark and the Fargo bunch went to Nashville, she would have to stay behind. Shelly, voiced her concern to Clark. He reminded her,

YOU'RE MOVING WHERE?

that they could afford a full time nurse for Ellie, and Nashville wasn't all that far away.

Shelly was blubbering on the phone when she got Clark on the line. She told Clark between sobs that her Gran wasn't going to make it. She had had a massive stroke and was in a comma. The Doctor held no hope for Ellie. Life had run out for the ninety-one year old. Clark told Shelly, "As soon as we pack the motor home with gear, we'll head for home."

Fargo was at the end of a three state dance hall tour, and pretty tired of it all. Clark needed to talk to Rick again about Chet Atkins and that tape of his he was supposed to send off. These dances, come-concerts, made money for the outfit, but were a lot of hard work. There were also the dead spots in the tour from Sunday till Thursday.

The boys took up basketball. They talked Clark into mounting a hoop on the back of the motor home. If they were back there playing, you didn't want to be in the motor home. It was far too noisy.

When Clark arrived at the Hospital, Shelly fell in his arms and really let emotions go. All that was left to do was unplug Ellie from life support. Clark didn't recognize Ellie. A big machine surrounded her bed, and in the middle was shriveled up little Ellie. Clark couldn't hold back the tears any longer. He wished he had spent more time with this dear old person. Life being the way it was had prevented that. Now it was too late. He held her hand and said, "Goodbye old friend, have a good trip."

He walked away with Shelly trailing behind him. The Doctor led them to a small waiting room, and sat down. Shelly and Clark sat down as well. He said there is no reason to keep her on life support any longer. Clark and Shelly nodded their heads and Shelly said, "Turn it off please; she's not here any longer."

CHAPTER 17

The house looked funny jacked up on dollies to carry it to its new home. Clark and Shelly looked on with mixed emotion as the huge prime mover moved the house at a snail's pace from its former foundation, headed for a new one.

After Ellie's funeral the Fargo's had completely renovated the old farm house. Now it didn't even resemble the old house. Clark and Shelly moved in and set up housekeeping. Four weeks later Shelly announced that she was pregnant and made Clark let go with a rebel yell that would have been heard by the neighbors, if they had had any.

Clark tried to pamper Shelly, but she stopped him with a hug and told him, she was a healthy person and not that far along yet, and could do for herself.

Clark, Doc, Brad, and Duke, were working on a newly written song, when Shelly and little three year old Clark the third came in the studio/garage, and announced there was a man here from the city to see him. The fellow was right behind Shelly and Clark could see he had his attention focused on his wife's posterior and not much else. Clark pulled him up from whatever his fantasy was at the moment with; "What can I do for you mister?"

The guy had been caught in the act, and grew red in the face. He began to stutter, caught himself and, said, "My name is Doland Wilks. I'm an attorney for the city of Macon, and I need to talk to you and your wife. Here his face turned crimson once more, I have business to conduct with the two of you. Clark thought; yeah I'll bet you do.

Clark and Shelly took Mr. Wilks over to the main house and went into Clark's office. After they were seated, Mr. Wilks said, "There is a huge shopping mall being built at this location, and your twelve acres are dead in the center of it. We must buy it from you in order to build the mall."

There was dead silence from Clark and Shelly. They were stunned by the horrible news. They had spent a lot of money on this house to update it to modern day relevance. Now this yo, yo, was sitting here and destroying their dream. Clark asked; "What if we don't want to sell? What then?"

YOU'RE MOVING WHERE?

Mr. Wilks had seen it all before, so he tried to be gentle with the two young people. He said, "Unfortunately the City will acquire the property by eminent domain, unless you sell at market value. You'll get much more money by letting us pay a negotiated price. The eminent domain order would mean far less money in your pocket."

Clark said, "Let us think about it for a few days, leave your number and I'll call you."

Wilks said, "We must put a time limit on this. If you don't call my office by this same day next week, we'll proceed with eminent domain. I'm sure we can come up with a settlement before then."

He got up and was about to turn away when, Shelly asked, "What will be done with the house?"

Doland always dreaded this part of his job. He said, "A bull dozer will push it down and crawl over it until it's in small enough pieces to be loaded on dump trucks and taken to the land fill."

Shelly was horrified that her Gran's house was bound for the dump. Doland liked the next part of his job. He said, "There is a way to save this nice house, we pay you market price for it, and you buy it back for the cost of destroying it. Then we will give you ample time to haul it to new land somewhere. You keep your house and we save money, think about it."

Then he was gone. He knew he had left two people in turmoil, but they were reasonably intelligent, and would probably follow the main stream and come to the table with their minds made up to deal.

Now here they were. Ellie's house was on wheels and on the move. Shelly and Clark found a twenty acre plot north of town seven miles. The place was a rundown small twenty acre piece that had been part of a six hundred acre farm. Illness had whittled it down through the years, and the final blow came when the last son came down with cancer and died. His kids wanted no part of it, so Clark and Shelly got it for a thousand bucks an acre.

The place had a three hundred foot deep well that tasted sweet. The old house was too far gone to save. Clark contracted with a construction company to clean the property up and build a new foundation for Ellie's house. They were financially way out in front. Dolan Wilks had offered one million four hundred thousand. Clark knew this was a fair offer and accepted it and paid the forty thousand bucks for the house. It was worth it. He and Shelly had put three times that in the renovation of the place.

YOU'RE MOVING WHERE?

Once the place was all settled into and the Fargo bunch spruced it up, one would think the house had been there all its life. The garage and apartment had been restored to its previous condition and Duke had moved in with his wife Cindy.

Duke had met Cindy when the entire bunch had wound up at Red Lobster for a feed. The three musicians called their singer and wife, and asked them to come out and eat with them. Shelly, Clark Jr and Clark Sr pulled into the parking lot of Red Lobster and saw the black mustang already there. After they took their seats with the boys, the little waitress popped up and said to Clark, "My name is Cindy and I'll be your server and take care of all your needs."

She was flirting shamelessly with Clark. Shelly turned slightly red, and she quipped, "He is mine, and I take care of all his needs."

Then in her deepest Georgia drawl she added, "Honey you serve the food and leave the rest to me, OK?"

Clark looked at Shelly and was so tickled he was losing it. Cindy put her nose in the air and with their food order in hand, kept it there all the way to the kitchen. When Cindy returned with their food order, she was much subdued.

Undaunted, she turned on Duke Fetcher and began her brand new campaign to win some man's heart. Old Duke {26} fell for her like a ton of cow crap. She successfully wrapped Duke in an inescapable web, and before the night was over, the two only had eyes for each other. It had taken only a short time before Duke committed himself for life.

After the wedding, Shelly and Clark insisted the couple move in the garage apartment. Cindy turned out to be a real nice girl from Oklahoma. She was part Indian and came from the Potter bunch up around Tulsa. Her home life hadn't been very pleasant as a child. She had been on her own since she turned sixteen; she was twenty-two now and the entire Fargo group fell in love with her. Duke was like a new man. Cindy was everything he dreamed of in a woman, and found her funny and easy to talk to.

YOU'RE MOVING WHERE?

CHAPTER 18

Clark was disgusted with music for the first time in his twelve years in the business. Rick Mosman was trying to soften the blow of Clark's unsuccessful bid to join the country music circle in Nashville. Rick said, "I did the best I could Clark. Chet never listened to our tape; he told me his roster is full for the foreseeable future. It makes me mad as hell, because I know you're a better singer then most of the ones making hits in music town. I tell you what I'd do if I was in your place. I would change countries in a heartbeat. I think you have plenty; money, talent, and charisma to pull it off in, say, England, Or Australia. Think about it. I don't think the TV show is a viable option any longer, because things are different now. You don't have to sell out here like most people do when they leave, keep what you have and move you, your family, and band somewhere other than a country where only a few die hard old hillbillies control what American's hear on the air waves."

Clark looked at Rick with new respect, and then said, "Rick, You have gone to the real problem I face, in an eloquent manner. Thank you for having faith in me and my music, you are a hundred percent right, and, It's up to me to do something about it, and I will."

There was stunned silence from the entire Fargo bunch. Clark had just lowered the boom on them and told them they were moving their music operation to Sydney Australia. Duke exclaimed, "We're moving where?"

Clark smiled and said, "Only those that want to play music down under with clean records can go"

No one is being forced to go. I must take my music as far as possible. I'm sure there will be replacements over there for anyone who wants to stay behind. This caused everyone to talk at once. Clark held up his hands and said," One at a time, please."

Duke stood and asked, "How do we pickers afford a move like that?"

Clark said, "Most of you have been with us for a number of years, and as you must know Shelly and I have been blessed with a considerable inheritance from Ellie. Your expenses will be our responsibility. You will also be paid tour wages for each show we book. For

YOU'RE MOVING WHERE?

you it's a win, win trip. If things go wrong, Hell, We'll just pack up and return home."

There was jubilation among the pickers then, because it was a pickers dream to tour Australia. Duke was the only long face Clark saw. He asked Duke what the problem was. Duke came back with, "What about my wife"?

Shelly piped up and said, "She goes with us Duke and we can't go until after Little Angelia, turns two. She would be a hand full right now. Next year will be soon enough."

Shelly was talking about the little eighteen month old blond headed angel that had the full attention of the bunch now, and already was a ham at this young age. Clark said, "I want to move my parents up here to look after the place while were gone. They can move in with us just before we leave. That will be in June. The winter months over there start then, and we won't burn our butts off when we land."

The next six months were the busiest in the Fargo's life. Not only did they have shows to do, Clark and Shelly decided to turn their twenty acres into a truck farm, which Clark's father Diller, would take over the management of. Diller and Ruby were dying to come back to Macon to live. They sold the mobile home, and arrived in late March. A happy reunion ensued, with a huge barbeque, and lots of country music, thrown in. As Rick Mosman, remarked, "Man, you're pretty popular here maybe you shouldn't go to Australia after all."

When Clark heard Rick say this he chided Rick, saying. "Look Rick, where we are going was your suggestion, I hope you make up your mind, I will tell you this; if you try to change our minds now you won't be popular with the band. Too much work has gone in getting accepted by the Aussies, for us to pull out at this stage."

Only one snag had been encountered getting the paper work done on his crew and family to enter Australia as immigrants. Each person must go through a stringent police background check. Old Duke flunked out because of a DWI while he was in the Army. It cost him a stripe and two month's pay. It was entered in his military records that were shipped to FBI headquarters at Langley. Langley then made them available to all police forces across the USA. Fortunately, Duke didn't lie about it and when, the consulate general saw who he was, he offered them a way around the obstacle. They would be willing to except a waiver on the matter and make a ruling as soon as possible.

CHAPTER 19
SYDNEY

The huge 747 arrived over Sydney Australia too early to land. There was a noise law enforcement until seven AM. The pilot came on and said, "Ladies and gentleman we have an hour to waste before we are able to set down, so I think a little aerial sightseeing tour is in order."

The pilot kept up a running commentary for most of the hour, then landed the plane with a slight bump as they touched down. As the plane taxied to the terminal, flight attendants sprayed disinfectant up and down the aisle. No deadly bug would be coming with them to this country.

There were representatives from the Australian government on hand to escort them. Only as a curtsy, they were told. Clark took the two aside and told them while this wasn't his first trip over, he wanted to find his own way and would lead his band to the Wentworth Hotel at Kings Cross, where they had reservations, made days ago from back home. The men looked like they had been kicked.

Clark felt sorry for them and told the two men they should come to one of their shows and inform the person taking tickets, to contact him back stage for free passes for them and their families. This mollified the two public servants, and they went away happy; while the Fargo bunch piled in four taxies and stormed Kings cross.

Clark and Shelly went house hunting. The hardest thing for the bunch to become accustomed, to was looking the wrong way and damn near getting wiped out by a car coming from the other way. "They drive on the wrong side of the road over here," Clark JR declared.

Shelly held the two children's hands, and stayed behind Clark as they crossed streets. Clark called a car rental company and was told the best thing for their safety was a chauffeur driven car. The chauffeur would act as a guide around Sydney as well.

The car company was a short ride from the hotel in a taxi, the car would arrive within ten minutes. The family of four waited in the lobby for the driver. Shortly, a cute pug nosed young girl came up to them, speaking in a soft burr of Scottish lilted English, she said, "Ye moust be the Fargo's I'm sure of it. Me names Tilly Bonifay

YOU'RE MOVING WHERE?

Mc-Rowen. If I be suitable for ye as yoor driver then we can be on our way."

This girl had a bubbly bright personality that entrapped the entire bunch in an instant. The two children went to her and took procession. They instantly belonged to Tilly and Tilly belonged to them as well. Shelly and Clark understood this. They were equally spell bound by this little beauty. Clark told the bunch, "Let's go before she decides were not worth bothering with."

Tilly got tickled at this and hugged the two kids to her.

Tilly was a delight; she was an encyclopedia when it came to Sydney, Australia, and kept the Fargo's entertained like no other had for years. Both children sat as close to her as was possible and still allow her to drive the car. As they approached Bondi Beach, four year old Clark Jr said. "Oooo Mommy, look at all the naked women."

Shelly grew red in the face, and told Tilly, that they had seen enough of Bondi beach for one day, thank you. Clark had to turn away, so Shelly couldn't see him smile.

Tilly took them out the highway north and back along the north Sydney beach highway. She told Clark he should see an estate agent to find a rental. Clark told her, "Take us to one."

Tilly turned off the road into a mall, and drove to an estate agent office. Clark and Shelly went in, leaving Tilly and the kids in the car.

The man who met them was dressed in white shirt and tie with shorts as pants. He said, "Good day mate, how can I help you two?"

Clark said, "We need to rent someplace for our family." The man introduced himself as Ian, and yes he had a list of rentals they could look through. He added, "If you tell me what your needs are, it might expedite the process."

Clark said, "I'm a country music singer, and I have my entire band to accommodate, so the place must be big, and we will pay a year's rent in advance."

Ian loved country music and was a fan of Reg Lindsey, one of the premier recording artists in Australia. He liked this big man from Georgia, and thought Shelly was the most beautiful woman he had ever salivated over. He asked, "Would you want to live on the north beach?"

Shelly and Clark both nodded their heads "yes."

Ian said, "Well this may well be your lucky day mate, I have a place a few miles from here that has over five thousand square feet of living space. The owner went back to the old country for a visit and fell ill, and is not well enough to make the return trip. Now he will rent it cheap I

YOU'RE MOVING WHERE?

think. If you want, I'll give you the key, with a map, and you can go look to your heart's content."

The Fargo's gave the map to Tilly and she took off back up the beach road. She found the place with no problem. They sat and looked at what appeared to be a mansion. Shelly asked, "Do you think we can afford that big of a place?"

Clark said, "Let's take a look and see."

They pulled up to the four car garage, and all got out. Clark unlocked the huge oak door and it silently opened with no noise. The interior smelled a bit musty but not unpleasant. They filed into the house. The thing was a mansion inside as well. Clark said, "Holy cow maybe we can't afford this."

He saw a phone and picked up the receiver, surprisingly there was a dial tone. He dialed the estate agents number on his card. Ian picked right up. After telling him who he was, he said, "You had better let me know what price range we're looking at here, before we go farther Ian."

Ian said, "The owner gave me lots of latitude on this house. It's too big for most renters. Why don't you take a good look at the place and then come and talk with me. I'm almost certain a deal can be worked out."

Clark hung up and they went from room to beautiful room. There were two kitchens, a small dining room off the smaller kitchen and a formal dining room that seated twenty people. Man, What a place. The living room was damn near big enough to play ball in. Upstairs they found five bed and three bath rooms, one was the master suite with its own bathroom, and the other two bathes were shared two rooms to a bath. The bathrooms were so very different than they were accustomed to, like not one of them had ever pulled a chain to flush a toilet in their lives. The two children went from bathroom to bathroom pulling chains. The carpet was so thick one couldn't hear their step, and the two kids sounded muted with their enthusiastic description of all they saw. Back down stairs they went out the back way and found an empty swimming pool with a chain link fence around it. Clark noticed the building protruded forty feet out past the rear door they had come out. Clark went back inside and looked for a door to that extra building. He found it in the small kitchen at the rear of the house. It was a main door, and was unlocked. The five of them trouped into one of the coziest three bedroom apartments they had ever seen. There was a door leading to another one car garage on the side of the house. Clark told Shelly let us go and talk to the man, we need this place.

YOU'RE MOVING WHERE?

Ian knew he had it rented the minute he saw the five enter his office. He wanted these folks in that house and his client over in Italy was needing the income. Clark said, "Tell me now how much per year."

Ian wrote some figures on his pad. Then he said, "Since the pool in unserviceable, I think forty eight hundred dollars annually would be a good deal for you. What do you think?"

Clark was a pretty good business man and said, "Make it American dollars, and we have a deal."

Ian thought, "This fellow will do ok here in Australia." He wrote down some more figures and said I think that thirty three hundred dollars Australian would be ok. Clark took out his check book and wrote the check for thirty three hundred dollars and no cents. He handed it to Ian, and said, "We transferred funds into this account some time ago, please call the bank and confirm the funds are available."

Ian was on the phone for less than a minute, and was all smiles when he hung up, He had made a good bit of money this day. He would take his twelve percent right off the top and deposit the rest in his client's account.

He told his new renters he would have the standard lease drawn up in an hour for their signatures. There would be no damage deposit because the owner had full insurance on the place, and if they damaged the place they would have an insurance company to deal with. Clark thought that was a neat way to do a rental. Ian said, "You should go to the electricity commission straight away and have them to read the meter, you won't be held responsible, for any use before now."

Clark said, "Point me at the place."

Tilly piped up and said, "I know where it is."

Shelly said, "Let's go."

Back at the Wentworth the band was looking forward to some Kings Cross night life, but after they heard about their new house however, everyone changed their minds, jumped in a taxi, and followed them north to the mansion with a full view of the mighty Pacific Ocean. Duke and Cindy got the one suite master bed room. Brad and Doc chose a bedroom each on the same side so as to have their own bathrooms. Clark and his family took the apartment.

Clark had had the phone put in his name, so he called the moving company and told them they could drop their stuff off anytime. The mover said he would bring it early next morning to please have someone available to show the drivers where to unload.

YOU'RE MOVING WHERE?

CHAPTER 20

1972 was a good year for country music in down under Australia. Radio 2Ky Country played country 24/7. Coll Beigent was the ramrod there and, when Clark called him he realized this man loved American Country Music. He agreed to meet with Clark and help him get started out right over here. Coll was impressed with Clark, who brought his acoustic guitar along, after Clark cut loose with some of the songs he wrote Coll become excited. When he was finished singing Coll said, "Man! You can really sell a song. I think you and your band should come out to the Country Music Spectacular being held at the north Sydney Fair grounds on the twenty-fourth of August. There should be a great crowd, and you will meet some top line entertainers."

Tilly was an absolute delight. The boy's Doc and Brad made a play for her and she brushed them off like the ever present sheep fly. The two boys' were hurt a bit, but soon were involved with other girls. They knew there were two women to each man in this country, and they were making the most of it.

Clark and Shelly asked Tilly would she mind if they called the rental company and had her and her car assigned for a month 24/7. Tilly was excited and told them oh please do, I love to drive you about our country When Clark called Tilly's company they said. "You have it mate. Have her drive you here and sign the papers."

The two children were ecstatic, they ran and hugged Tilly.

After signing the paper work and paying in advance The Singer and his wife and children went shopping. Tilly drove them out southwest to Parametta. There were miles of new and used cars and trucks on either side of the road. Clark asked Tilly what kind of a car they were riding in. She told him, "It is a Holden, and was the only car made by Australian's."

Clark said. "Take us to that dealer."

Tilly drove for about a mile, and then turned in at a sign with a lion depicted with the word, "Holden" on it.

Shelly saw their family car across the showroom floor, and led the bunch plus one excited sales person straight to a burgundy colored station wagon. The salesman knew these people had money. It was written all over them. They were Americans and he loved

YOU'RE MOVING WHERE?

Americans. Clark opened the left door and sat down. He exclaimed. "Damn, someone stole the steering wheel."

There were peals of laughter from the rest of the bunch. Clark said," Hell, they brought it back and installed it on the wrong side of the damn car."

By this time the salesman was so tickled he almost lost it. Clark said, "We'll take it anyhow. I can learn to drive on the wrong side of the road. Tilly here will teach me."

He finally got the salesman settled down and asked him his name. The fellow was Jon Beardly. He wrung Clark's hand like it was pump handle. Clark wrote a check for three thousand and ninety eight dollars Australian and asked Jon if he could see the car delivered to their home in north Sydney. Jon said," Don't worry mate, I'll clear this check and bring it around later this afternoon."

Clark asked where he could find new step vans. Jon said, "Our truck lot is around back, on a different street. I'll take you there through our fence now."

He took off almost at a run. He wanted this commission too. They went through a gate in the fence and suddenly they were engulfed by trucks of all kinds. Clark saw what he was looking for. A row of bread truck type vehicles were on the back fence. They all walked down the row looking at vans of all description. He saw the one that would do, and zeroed in on it. The van was blue in color, and was about thirty feet long. He thought this thing will cost more than the station wagon. Much to his surprise Jon said, "This is last year's model and has a price on it that reflects that. You can buy it for twenty-eight hundred dollars out the door."

Clark set in it and fired the six cylinder engine up, it purred like a well-oiled machine. He said, "We'll take it, and you can deliver it as well."

Tilly took them shopping at David Jones department store not far from their home. Shelly almost bought the store out. Clark sure was glad David Jones delivered to your home.

Clark and Shelly were surprised at the variety on the grocery shelf. There were some things they had never seen before. Tilly tried to explain what each item was. The strangest was Vegemite. Tilly said she had it on toast each morning. Shelly grabbed the largest jar. It turned out later that the kids loved it, Shelly could take it or leave it, and Clark hated the stuff. He even told Shelly it looked like baby poop and for sure couldn't be fit to eat.

Tilly looked after the family as if they were her own, as a matter of fact she didn't have a

YOU'RE MOVING WHERE?

family. Her mother and father had brought Tilly to this country as a two year old in the early fifties and settled in Sydney. Her father had been conscripted into the Australian Army in 1964 and was shipped to Vietnam with the Australian contingent, at Dac Doctar rubber tree plantation, west of Saigon. He was killed during a rocket attack on the Australian base there.

Tilly was thirteen and totally devastated by his death. Her mother fainted when told the bad news, and had to be attended to by a doctor for some days after. When Tilly turned fourteen she took a clerking job in a grocery store near her and her mother's flat. When she turned sixteen her mother died.

One afternoon she came home and found her mother sitting on the kitchen floor dead. She had had a massive heart attack and died before she hit the floor. Tilly was once more devastated. She and her mother were close and Tilly still missed her after all these years. She had turned twenty just before she met the Fargo's.

Shelly walked into the family room where Clark Junior, Angelia, and Tilly were putting a huge puzzle together. She looked at Tilly and noticed tears running down her cheeks, she exclaimed, "Tilly honey, what is the matter?"

Tilly really let go the water works then. She said in between sobs, "I have only four more days to be with this family and it's killing me. I love all of you so very much."

Shelly took Tilly in her arms and said, "I will see what we can work out; let me talk to Clark OK?"

Tilly bobbed her head and dried her eyes. She said, "It's so silly of me. I'm so sorry, please forgive me."

Shelly found Clark and the band in what was loosely referred to as the music room, the living room was huge and the band barely took up one corner of the thing. When Shelly walked in, Duke was playing "The Orange Blossom Special". When the number finished, Shelly asked Clark to come and talk with her. When she told him about Tilly, he become upset at himself for not doing what he was about to do, long before now. He and Shelly marched to the family room and Clark said, "Tilly, do you want to stay in our employment full time as driver, Nanny to our kids, and all around family member?"

Tilly breathlessly said without any hesitation whatsoever, "YES."

The Fargo's and Tilly were hugging and laughing then. After a bit, Clark asked Tilly, "How much do I have to pay you?"

Tilly replied with, "That's up to you, but not too much, you might spoil me."

YOU'RE MOVING WHERE?

Clark said, "Let's make it 100 dollars a week, but I want you to start a savings account down at our bank. It will be in yours and my name. I will put fifty dollars in your account each week and you will receive the other fifty in cash. Does that sound OK to you?"

Tilly said, "That's far too much sir."

Clark said, "We expect you to be with us a long time, and please don't call me sir."

Tilly ran and hugged Clark and Shelly. She said, "Ye ave made me an appy Scots girl ye ave." Her Scottish brogue was a soft burr, and very pleasant to listen to.

The twenty-fourth of August came in a blustery cold day. The fairgrounds on highway one north out of Sydney had an outdoor stage with crude backstage dressing rooms. When their driver [Duke] pulled the converted step van behind the stage area, there was a small crowd gathered around Col Beigent, who was talking to them with a clip board in his hands that he made notations on.

As the Fargo bunch descended from the van, Clark noticed a big tall fellow in black, with a white cowboy hat. He thought the man looked familiar, but turned when Coll came over and shook his hand. All of a sudden Clark yelled out loud, "By damn, it's Del Rivers."

The guy in black said, "Well I'll be, if it ain't Clark Fargo,"

The whole bunch let a rebel yell out and pandemonium broke out, Coll got out of the way. He was amazed; these two entertainers knew each other. Everyone was talking at once. Lots of back slapping and hugging was taking place as well. Del said, "I've wondered if you might come over here Clark. There's a lot of work as an entertainer in these slot machine Clubs here in New South Wales. There's about 1200 Clubs in Sydney alone that put on shows at least once a week, and a good many of them put one on two and three shows a week. You picked a great way to get started. Col Beigent is my agent, and he books me all over, and when he hears you sing he will do the same for you and your band, I think."

Clark asked Del how his family was and a cloud came over Del's face. Clark could have bit his tongue off. Del said," Well, you know how it was while I was in Vietnam Clark. It will never be the same between us again. She won't support my music, and never misses a chance to tell me, to go get a job."

I stay with her because of the kids, and when they're gone from home, then so am I."

Del led Clark over to a strapping young man that looked like him, and said, "This is my son

YOU'RE MOVING WHERE?

Buddy, Today is his twelfth birthday. He has turned out to be a pretty good picker, he will back me today on lead, he knows all my stuff back to front."

Clark shook Buddy's hand, and could tell he was a picker; his hand was soft and dry. Buddy was looking over at Brad, Doc, and Duke. Clark said, "Come on Buddy I'll introduce you to my band."

Buddy remembered the boys from the barbecue at the mobile home park back at Fort Rucker. They all shook hands. There was a black fellow there, and Col grabbed Del and took him to meet him. Col said, "Jimmy Little, meet Del Rivers from America."

Del had heard of Jimmy, he was a legend here in his native country. He had recorded a song called "Telephone to Glory" that climbed the charts and remained at number one for six weeks. The Aussies loved to compare their singers to other singers overseas and because Jimmy was black, they chose Nat King Cole as his likeness. All the news media referred to him as, Australia's Nat King Cole. Jimmy later told Del, he hated it.

Del went on first and warmed the crowd of three thousand fans of country up. His bracket ran twenty minutes. The band, were Australians, and were horribly out of tune due to the cold weather and warm fingers on strings. Del's son, Buddy, went around and tuned all the cheap instruments up as they played. In no time at all the band sounded good. Buddy did this while playing lead for his Dad. Del really fired then and when he finished the crowd was on their feet screaming for more. They wouldn't let him go, so he did the last verse of the last song again, then did the chores twice and left the stage.

Col was running around in circles, saying over and over again; I'll make them into stars. Jimmy was on next; he wrung Del's hand half off and said. "Don't go anywhere, I want to talk to you after I'm done."

Jimmy was no slouch, and did one of the best twenty minute shows Del had ever heard. He had grabbed Buddy and said, "Come play lead for me would you?"

Buddy said, "You bet I will sir."

The crowd loved it; history was being made right before their eyes; watching a twelve year old boy become a star. Clark thought; it couldn't get much better than this. Clark and his band were on after the break. At first, the reception wasn't real good, until Clark got into some of his songs he wrote, then the crowd warmed up and by the time he came off, he had them in his pocket. Del, Col, and Jimmy shook Clark's hand, and told him there wasn't a thing wrong with

YOU'RE MOVING WHERE?

what he did on stage. Jimmy little said, "You have an excellent band Clark that's hard to find anywhere."

Jimmy asked Del for his phone number, and what would be a good time for him to call. Del replied "Anytime, I don't work any other job so I'm home most of the time."

Jimmy little called Del Rivers on Monday afternoon, and the two of them talked eight hours on the phone. Del sipped on a bottle of Aussie blush the entire time, and when they finally broke the connection, Del could hardly stay on his feet on the way to his bed.

Del told Jimmy about it later and Jimmy said he had no idea Del was even drinking. They both had a laugh at that. Jimmy wanted Del to meet his wife, so Del invited them over for dinner on a Wednesday evening. Del and his wife Dide made the entertainer and his wife feel right at home. Del's wife was German and could really cook up a wonderful meal. Their company tore into the food like they hadn't eaten for a while. Jimmy said, "I don't remember enjoying a meal this much in years."

His wife Georgiana had a strange look on her face. Jimmy didn't realize that he had put his foot in a gob of pooh. Georgiana was silent for most of the rest of the meal. Del thought there might be trouble on down the road with Jimmy's other half.

After the meal, the two Singers moved into the living room for a talk. Jimmy asked Del if he would like to share the spotlight with him, on what was supposed to be an all black show. The musical director however was a white guy by the name of Steve; he was the keyboard player for Jimmy's Band. Del didn't even hesitate before he said, "You bet, if you think I'm good enough Jimmy."

Jimmy said, "I saw how you fared with that gig at the fairgrounds, and I hope I learn from you, how to do that."

CHAPTER 21

Clark said, "Hey! Come here and look at the TV."

The rest of the bunch made it at a run to see what Clark was watching. There was Del Rivers on the tube singing his heart out on a song called "Pan American", an old Hank Williams tune. Duke said, "He's sure breathing new life into that tune."

The rest said "Amen to that." Little Angelia was jumping up and down and pointing at the black and white TV. Saying, "Uncle Del, Uncle Del."

This caused them all to laugh out loud. Clark thought, Old boy, you are on your way now for sure. Del had told Clark the seven networks in New Castle, New South Wales, wanted him to appear on the Let's Go out West Show, with Rob Johnson, an up and coming singer as MC, but this was a pleasant surprise for all.

Clark called Del the next day and invited him and his family over for a Barbecue the following

Sunday. He told Del, Coll Beigent and his family were coming out as well. Del wanted Clark to invite Jimmy and his wife, but these were southern boys, and he didn't want to push him into something he might not feel like doing.

Clark cooked a quarter of a beef over the beautiful grill on the back patio. It had a rotating spit and as the beef cooked the aroma was wonderful. Clark bought two hundred pounds of charcoal for the occasion, and had built the fire at six am and was cooking by seven am.

Mountains of potatoes salad and a great pot of Boston baked beans, had been prepared by, Shelly, Tilly and Cindy the day before, and stored in the refrigerator to chill. Doc and Brad invited their current girlfriends and that made a lot of mouths to feed.

The entire thing was a resounding success, and wore the Fargo bunch to a frazzle. Shelly muttered to Clark that it was someone else's turn next time.

She and Clark hugged each other and laughed. A lot of good had been done on this day and deep down, they were proud they'd pulled it off so well. The rear quarter of a cow was mostly bone and there weren't any beans or potato salad left. At least no one went home hungry.

YOU'RE MOVING WHERE?

Clark and Del had a talk after the meal. Clark asked Del if he would like to join forces with the Fargo bunch, and put together a show for touring purposes. Del said, "Dang Clark, I was asked by Jimmy Little to Co-Star on his existing show, and I accepted. I'll work with you whenever I can, and I'll talk to Jimmy and maybe he will afford you the same opportunity."

Clark said, "That would be great Del, we'll compare booking dates from time to time".

Del said, "That TV show I did has been shown on fifty or more ABC affiliate stations across Australia, and it has turned me into pretty hot property. The thing is, Jimmy got me on that TV show, so I owe him for that. At the same time, I'll help you anyway I can buddy, remember that."

In May of 1975, Jimmy little phoned Del Rivers up all excited, telling him he had been contacted by Festival Recording with a cover song they wanted him to record for a quick release in Australia. The song was Baby Blue, recorded by a Dutch rock and roll group in New Zealand. Jimmy was excited because he didn't know how to do the song. He asked Del if he could show him how. Del told Jimmy he would have to re-write the thing before anyone could sing it.

It took Del two days to revamp the song. He learned the song and sang it for his son Buddy. Buddy thought it was great, so Del took it to Jimmy, who learned it and sang it like Del did. No matter; Festival loved it as well and assigned an A&R man that had recorded some hit rock and roll song over in England. He met Del and Del knew instantly this man didn't like Americans. Del took it all with a smile. The song would be cut at Col Joy's studio in Sydney.

When Jimmy and Del arrived at the studio, the English A&R man was strutting around like the only rooster in the pack. First up he said, "I've arranged the song in the key of "F."

Jimmy deferred to Del with a nod, and Del said, "That's too bad, because Jimmy does the song in G."

Just before the colonial war began all over once again, Jimmy stepped in and told ole Ding the song would be done in "G".

Ole Ding almost strangled at this turn of events, he stomped off without a word. The first cut was at break neck speed and almost comic at the discomfort Jimmy was experiencing. When the song ended, ole Ding said in an excited voice, "That was great Jimmy I think it's a wrap."

YOU'RE MOVING WHERE?

Jimmy looked at Del and motioned him aside for a conference. He said, "This is terrible, that guy is ruining your song."

Del asked him, "What do you want me to do Jimmy?"

Jimmy said, "Please intervene on my behalf."

Ole Ding knew we were discussing him, and was already puffed up with indignation when Del approached him with Jimmy at his side. Del said, "Firstly, Jimmy has just given me authorization to act as intermediary for the duration of this recording."

Ole ding became even more puffed up and said. "What did you say?"

Del said, "That cut stinks, and if you think it's good, you probably should return to England and make someone else miserable." He further added, "the song was recorded far too fast, shove that stop watch up your ass and let this artist have an opportunity to record his song at his speed and you just might learn something."

Del's friend Jimmy Little let loose, and put chill bumps all over all present except ole Ding, who threatened to walk out unless this damn Yank was removed from the session. Jimmy, in his quite gentle voice said, "If Del goes, so do I."

Del told Jimmy he had just made a great recording and he would be in the control room for the rest of the night.

The engineer named Bill gave Del the thumbs up and motioned him into the control room. He shook Del's hand and, said, "Thank goodness you were here, if you hadn't been, that damn Englishman would have ruined Jimmy Little's career for sure."

Bill asked Del if he drank at all. Del said, "I sure could use one after that fiasco."

Bill reached down and brought out a bottle of Jim Beam Kentucky bourbon whisky. He said, "There's ice and mix in that fridge right over there, and you can fix two of them, because I need one too. I thought you were gonna take that idiot out of the picture. I'm glad you put him in his place. Here's to you."

He held his glass up in salute and Del did the same.

As Del looked past Bill's hand out the window to the studio he caught Jimmy's eye through the window and Jimmy gave him a thumbs up. He knew Del drank some, but had never seen him take one until after the job was done, and Del had done one hell of a job here tonight.

The string section came in along with all other pieces and with Jimmy's excellent guide

YOU'RE MOVING WHERE?

vocal, the entire song was ready to mix before Del and Bill got too much alcohol in their system. The mix was the best Del had ever heard. He knew a hit when he heard one, and this song had hit sticking out all over it. Ole Ding had the last word. He stuck his head in and said, "You messed this recording all up, and I'm telling my boss Mr. Brown about it."

There was dead silence in the control room. Finally Ding couldn't stand it anymore and left as the three broke out in laughter.

At 10 AM the next morning, Del's phone rang. It was Jimmy, and he said, "Mr. Brown will see us at one O'clock in his office at Festival record company."

Del and Jimmy met in the parking lot and walked in thinking, maybe they were wrong and ole Ding was right about them, maybe it was a bad recording, and they were about to be canned. Del didn't much give a phizz, if it had to be done Ding's way, he wouldn't be in it anyhow. When they reached the reception area, they told the young lady who they were and that they had an appointment with Mr. Brown. Here was ole Ding pacing back and forth, like the only rooster in the hen house once more. He knocked on Mr. Brown's door and went in with Del and Jimmy close behind. Mr. Brown rose from his chair and came around to meet them, he zeroed in on Del first. He shook his hand and said, "It's a pleasure to meet you Del. I've heard good things about you from Jimmy and I'm sure they are true."

He then shook Jimmy's hand and said, "Thanks for coming in Jimmy, it's been too long, please sit down. How about some coffee?"

Jimmy declined, but Del was hung over and needed some pretty bad. Mr. Brown told Ding to get Mr. Rivers a cup of coffee. Ole Ding looked like he had been slapped, but he got up and left the office. He returned and set the cup on the desk. Del took a sip and set it down. The asshole had salted his coffee.

Mr. Brown asked Del, "Did you really drink half a bottle of whisky last night Del?" Before Del could respond, Ding piped up and said, "He sure did Mr. Brown!"

Brown held his hand up and said, "I was talking to Mr. Rivers do you mind?"

Ole Dings butt almost hit the floor. Del said, "If the truth be known sir, I feel more like I drank the whole damn thing. I want to apologize if I messed anything up last night."

Mr. Brown came back with, "I listened to the cut twice this morning, and it's absolutely the best thing Jimmy has ever done, and we are going to release it just like it is."

Ding stood up trembling like he was freezing. Just before he turned to leave, Del handed the

YOU'RE MOVING WHERE?

salted cup of coffee to him and said, "Take this salted cup of coffee with you and don't come around me anymore."

Ding slunk out of the office like the snake he was.

When "Baby Blue" was released it shot to number twelve and remained on the charts for six weeks. Jimmy was more popular than he had ever been. Del did about seventy-five shows with him as his Costar. Jimmy was a super star and the two would probably have been together longer if Jimmy's wife and Del hadn't gotten sideways with each other over her telling him what to do back stage. Del walked out just before a show in Sydney and never looked back. He had other options.

CHAPTER 22
UNITED WE STAND

Clark was glad to hear from Del Rivers. When he heard what happened with Jimmy, he said to Del, "Maybe you should join up with my outfit."

Del said, "Ok man; I'll come over and talk to you about what we should do, we Americans have to stick together, you know."

Clark said, "Come on over friend."

Del arrived at the Fargo house to a warm welcome. Tillie's heart did a little flip, but she didn't let it betray her at any time. They had a warm friendly get together. Del and Clark went off to another room to talk.

Del said, "I've worked real hard to do everything right over here, and consequently; I've attained a good following, especially in the small towns in the bush. I honestly feel we can use that as a vessel to launch a tour around this country that would not only be fun, but lucrative

YOU'RE MOVING WHERE?

as well. You are no slouch as an entertainer yourself and you have one of the best bands this country has ever seen. If you don't want to stay stuck in these poker clubs until you're old and gray, let's put a show together called Del Rivers and Fargo. I'll do promo through Coll Beigent and radio 2Ky Kountry. That should launch us all proper like. It means a trip around this country booking our own shows wherever we choose to be."

Clark was getting excited as Del laid out his plan, he had thought about it often. He said, "Let's go and put it to the rest of the gang."

Clark assembled the Fargo bunch in the huge dining room. After they were seated and settled down, he said, "Folks I want to know how you feel about a tour around Australia as Del Rivers and Fargo."

Clark couldn't believe the cheer that went up from everyone at his question. He sat down and smiled at Del. "There's your answer my good friend and star of your own show."

Del Rivers and Fargo was a hit with the people from the get go. The insurmountable problem was their confrontation with the almost communist actor's equity union. Del and Clark were summoned to meet a representative in their office in downtown Sydney. Within two minutes, they both knew this man hated anything

American, and he wasn't about to make an exception for them. His statement went something like this; "We don't need you Americans coming over here taking money from our performers. We have enough talent in this country, and, if you show here in this city we will demand 50% of your receipts as union dues, or you won't work. We will shut down any club that books you that doesn't pay up front as well."

Del and Clark sat with their chins on the floor. This was impossible to comprehend, what was wrong with this guy. Clark regained his composure first, and said, "You are out of your friggin mind."

Del, finally spoke, and said, "You asshole".

The two walked out with asshole screaming at their backs. On the way to Clark's car, Del said, "Well, I supposed we will go on extended tour around this country a bit sooner than I thought we would."

Clark said, "You're damn right. We will book halls and theaters all about the country, and be phantoms the union can't put their finger on. Then by damn I'm going back home, where I'm a first class citizen."

Del stopped and turned to Clark, and said, "Don't leave me here and you need to fix Tilly up so she can migrate to the USA."

YOU'RE MOVING WHERE?

Clark looked at Del, but didn't comment. He knew Del and Tilly were attracted to one another, but Del took his vows to his wife to heart, and never once took advantage of Tilly. Del knew his wife would never leave Australia, because he had discussed the possibility of returning to the US, and working as an Entertainer there. She had said, "Flat no!"

Clark thought Del just might be thinking about down the road a bit, and Clark didn't blame him one bit.

CHAPTER 23
THE AUSSIE HIGHWAY EXPRESS

Del chose Beaudesert Queensland as their first show booking. He told Clark they were out of poker machine territory up here, and would more than likely, not be of any interest to the union this far north. They had plenty of funds available, thanks to Clark, so if they didn't make a killing it wouldn't break them. Everyone would work anyway.

There were a million things to do before the show date, and all hands pitched in to do whatever. Del believed in the old fashion way to promote a show. Just like politicians did it. The Fargo bunch would canvass their prospective fans and entice them to buy tickets for the show. The kids, Del's and Clark's, must deliver color posters to as many people as they could meet each day.

A great deal of work went into getting this show on the road. They picked a non school period to launch the show. Shelly and Del's wife

YOU'RE MOVING WHERE?

arranged to home school all the kids. This left them with no tether to hold them back. The only unhappy one was Del's wife, Dedi, who didn't support Del's music and would rather have stayed home. Del and Clark talked about the situation. Clark said, "I can see you aren't your normal self Del. I can't advise you on what to do, but I'm here to help if I can."

Del was touched; Clark sure had turned out to be a real friend. He said, "I'll sort something out, thanks for your support."

They sold 2400 advanced tickets, and another 1200 showed up at the booth attended by Duke's wife Cindy. She was everyone's choice as the gate watcher. Just before showtime, Del received a frantic phone call from Cindy. She said, "I have two really surly characters down here saying they're union representatives, and I should let them in free. I've informed them if they buy a ticket, I'll gladly let them in. They requested I contact the Boss of the show, and you're it."

When he reached the front of the huge hall, Del found the two union rep's damn near foaming at the mouth. They were incensed that a little girl just over a hundred pounds had held them at bay. Del took the two in, at one glance. They had trouble written on every part of their body. He said softly, "And now just what can I do for you fellows?"

The silence hung in the air like fog. The tallest one stepped up to Del and looked up at his face, and said, "We are here to collect union dues from you for your show tonight."

Del, still in a soft voice said, "And just how much is that sir?" The man said, "That depends on how much you took in at the box office, we need 25% of that."

This was extortion and Del knew it. He said, "Come with me and I'll pay you."

He walked out and didn't care much if they followed him or not. When he reached his big long Van he knocked on the door, and Dedi let him in. The two Rep's tried to follow him in but Del put his hand on the first ones chest and gently but firmly pushed him and his partner backwards and closed the door.

He heard the both of them hit the ground with a smack and much cursing. He did a quick calculation of how much he owed them and wrote a check for the amount. He went to the door and stepped out. The rep's were leaning on his car, but bolted towards him when they saw him. He handed the check to the tall one, and the man said, "We don't accept checks mate, you must pay in cash."

YOU'RE MOVING WHERE?

Del reached and took the check back and put it in his front shirt pocket. He said, "Meet me at the bank of New South Wales tomorrow morning and I'll give you cash."

As he started walking off, the two attempted to block his way. Del in his soft southern drawl said, "You really don't want to do that. Just meet me at the bank here in Beaudesert at 11 AM, and you will get your money."

The two thugs thought they had about run this creek dry, so they backed off and walked away. The show went well and everyone went home a fan.

The following day, Del and Clark waited at the bank until twelve noon, no union rep showed up to claim the money. Del told Clark he didn't think they would either.

Clark said, "Those two must be crooked to not claim the money."

Del said, "Yeah, feel like a trip to Brisbane?"

They had to ask directions three times before they parked in the union parking lot. Inside, the receptionist was a nice brown headed young girl. She was friendly and open as Del explained who he was. When he finished she said. "OK how much did you gross"?

When Del told her, she said. "We take 5%, do you want to pay now or send it later"?

Del said, "We'll pay now."

He and Clark exchanged looks. After they paid, Del asked the girl, "Is there a manager handy that we could have a word with?"

The girl said, "Sure let me tell him you want to see him."

Del and Clark liked the fellow instantly. He got up and met them, and shook hands. He said, "I'm sure glad to meet you Del, I've been a fan since watching you on TV."

Del was taken back a bit. This was not the treatment he was used to receiving from the union. The man said, "I sent two reps out to Beaudesert to welcome you, did you meet them?"

Del said in his soft voice that could hit high "C" in a song with ease, "Yes they wanted to charge us this amount".

He handed the voided check to the rep. the rep stood up and called his receptionist. He said, "June call the police for me and tell them an extortion attempt has been made. We need a detective down here to talk to two witnesses before they have to return home."

He hung the phone up, then said, "I apologize, these two have done some questionable deeds before, but this time we have the goods on them. This union is an entertainers advocate, and not in bed with any

YOU'RE MOVING WHERE?

crooks. They were supposed to charge you 5% and no more."

The police arrived and took everything down. The cop said, "I think we have enough to make an arrest. I want to think you so very much, and hope I can see your show someday".

He shook hands all around, then left.

Fargo, with Del Rivers was a great combo. The shows were easy to book and promote. They played to packed or near packed house's as far north as Townsville out on the coast.

Del had heard Shelly and Angelia sing and had wondered when they would break out and sing on stage. It was there in Townsville that Shelly and Angelia broke into show biz. Del was doing one of his favorite tunes; "The Green, Green Grass Of Home', when he had a shiver run up his spine. He half turned and there was the mother and daughter singing their hearts out. Del did the resuscitation, and turned and said into the microphone, "Ladies and gentleman, making their début on stage, two of the most beautiful women I know. They are the wife and daughter of my friend and costar Clark Fargo. Make welcome, the lovely Shelly Fargo and her Daughter Angelia."

Del whispered to Clark to kick off "Funny Face", a recent hit for Donna Fargo (no relation) over in the states. The crowd was silent throughout the entire song. Most of them had their mouths to fall open. These two gals could sell a song. When they finished, the crowd came to their feet screaming for more. Clark had tears of happiness running down his cheeks. The girls had to sing more of the song to quiet the crowd down. They got another standing ovation, and left the stage. Del decided to end the show five minutes early and devote the time to singing a long version of, "Will The Circle Be Unbroken". It was the most fitting song he could think of, and it got the two new stars out to sing their hearts out through the whole song.

The show had grown by twenty percent with the addition of the female duet, and improved by a much greater percentage. Del was used to working with back-up singers. He told Clark it made his job more pleasurable, knowing those two would be there each time he did his part on the show.

Mount Isa Queensland is a copper mining town about 275 miles northwest of Townsville. It can be easily distinguished by its 500 foot red and white tower pipe at the copper smelter. In theory this pipe took the deadly smelter fumes far enough up in the sky so no one had to breathe the foul stuff. It didn't work for the most part. The wind would whip the stuff around and everyone had to breathe the green crap anyhow.

YOU'RE MOVING WHERE?

It was hard on the Del Rivers show bunch. Everyone felt like they were coming down with a bad cold. The smoke played hell with older folk's sinus passages. Del suffered most, simply because he was the oldest one there. The night of their show, Del apologized to the audience for sounding like a bull elephant and with their permission he would have to clean his airways out after each song. He made a comical thing out of it, with exaggerated nose blowing. The fans ate it up. The show was a success, with 2200 fans going home happy.

CHAPTER 24

The heat was like a white searing pain in one's eyes in Darwin Northern Territory. The humidity pressed in on them like some hot smothering blanket, twenty-four hours a day. The City rested a thousand miles south of the equator. It was no wonder people committed suicide each October by leaping off the water tower. The tower was known around Darwin as Tropo leap and to date, had claimed 278 victims.

They showed at the Fairgrounds, and parked their Vans in one of the empty pavilions. That kept the bugs off them but it was hotter than red chile peppers. The two vans everyone slept in were air conditioned. Duke and Cindy traveled in an 18 foot camping trailer that had no air conditioner, so Del and Duke went down and bought one and installed it. It was hard on everyone doing three hours under the bright lights of the stadium.

They got it done however and left the hot town of Darwin the next morning. It was winter time up here. Del and Clark both agreed, they would sure hate to be here in the summer.

The road south and west was all dirt or gravel, with dangerous pot holes that threatened to swallow a car or van up. Near the small towns, the roads improved dramatically for the show's caravan of vehicles. There were always things to be welded, replaced, or repaired in each town they arrived at. Tires were their main problem, and weren't always available. They had to be ordered in from Sydney. This took anywhere from one week to three weeks. In Broom, Western Australia They needed seven tires that were questionable for the two main vans. Clark, as was his job, was told they had exhausted the supply of that size tire in Australia, and the tires would have to be shipped from England. There was no telling how long this might take, so Del and Clark decided to book two shows in the town.

Del was told, this was a mining town and they should have one show that catered to the night shift and one for the day shift. The town of Broom rolled out the carpet for the Fargo bunch. Del spent a lot of time down at the Hotel's pub. No women were allowed, and he could escape Dedi's constant complaining about everything in general, but mainly, why was she being subjected to the harsh conditions out here, when they had a comfortable home back in Sydney.

Del finally bent to her wishes and put her and the four kids on a plane to Perth WA and then on to Sydney. He was on his own now and knew he would never live with Dedi again. Del missed his children, and he lost himself in that pub. He would still promote the two shows they booked however and always took his guitar to the pub and sing for the folks there and in the lounge. There were ladies in the lounge that found him irresistible, but he was so miserable over his children, he never returned their advances. Del was kinda fond of Tilly, but didn't want to compromise his and the Fargo's working relationship. He was always nice and friendly towards her and she returned that friendliness, but that was as far as it went. Clark, Shelly, Duke, Cindy, the two kids, and Tilly flew back to Sydney to close the house down, and ship their house goods over to Perth.

Del, Brad, and Doc had hellacious parties while the Fargo's were gone and with no other seeing eyes on them, divulged themselves with female company from time to time. There were plenty of girls about, but Del mostly found one he could talk to, and still didn't take her to his van. Hell he didn't even know why. What was wrong with him? He supposed he had really tried to make his marriage work, and when he couldn't, it must have messed his mind up a bit. He would get back in the saddle once again with time.

CHAPTER 25
THE ROAD HOME

The two shows were as successful as could be expected with a double booking. Over half of the seats were filled at each show. On the final night, Del told the fans they were returning to the USA on the Marine Shipping Lines. They had booked passage on the Dutch freighter and passenger liner Bostich; she sailed on the tenth of June out of Perth Western Australia. There was an audible sigh from the audience. Some guy jumped up and said, "You're welcome back over here anytime mates."

Del had been on big ships before, and the ups and downs didn't bother his stomach, but the rest of the bunch consisting of the Fargo's and Tilly along with Duke and Cindy were sea sick before they were out of sight of land. Doc and Brad chose to fly home. Tilly was the most pathetic one, the poor girl was hurling over the fantail almost constantly. Del had anticipated this and took her a full box of saltine crackers and told her to munch on them. The next day Tilly was able to stay away from the fantail, however she remained a bit green about the gills for another day. After that she began to enjoy the cruise somewhat. She handed crackers out to everyone and looked at Del with calf eyes. Shelly seemed to be the only one to notice and thought, "Del Rivers, you have captured my Tillie's heart, you big lug, and you won't do anything about it, because you are too much of a gentleman." Shelly thought about talking to Clark about it, but didn't want to meddle in Del's affairs. It might push him to do something he's not ready for.

The six week boat trip, while necessary to transport their vehicles and house hold goods home, was a long and mostly hot uncomfortable affair. The only relief from the relentless sun was below deck. The cabins and lounges were air-conditioned and comfortable, although cramped. They found no interest in their music from any of the passengers or crew, who were mostly Philippinos and seriously went about their business.

Del was probably the most miserable one of the bunch. He missed his children like mad, and knew he probably wouldn't see them for a long time. This made him haunt the ship in search of something that wasn't there; he graduated to the ship's bar, to sit on a stool with his guitar and a cold beer. Duke knew his friend was going through some hard times, and with Cindy's blessings sat and played fiddle with Del. The little Pilipino girls would pass through the lounge and make eyes and giggle at the two cutting up on song after song.

The Bostich berthed in Seattle Washington on the 25th of august 1978. The Fargo bunch felt like kissing the ground when they set foot on shore, tears rolled down Shelly's cheeks. She hadn't realized how much she missed the states in the seven years they'd been gone. Del had been gone for nine years, and he misted up as well.

Clark and his family, along with Tilly, Duke and Cindy, took off in the direction of home, while Del went south to Portland, where he had family. He would then go down to California and play music with folks he'd known there, from a long time ago. Del promised the Fargo's he would stay in contact. Shelly said, "You had better, you have people here who think more of you then you think."

Del knew Shelly was talking about Tilly, but didn't respond in any way, he had too many things on his mind and couldn't see that far in to his murky future.

YOU'RE MOVING WHERE?

The place was packed on this Saturday night. The band was Gene Moles, and the Mole Bunch. Gene was a good friend of Merle Haggard, and had played on many of the great man's recordings. The Best Western Lodge in Bakersfield, was Gene's normal Saturday night gig, and this was one of the better ones. He supposed the audience had had a good pay day.

Gene heard a commotion near the entrance door and glanced over. This giant of a man in a mauve colored suit with black vents at the ankles and wrists was standing with a guitar slung across his back Cash style. Del had his thumbs hooked in his belt and his suit jacket was open. His frilly shirt front gleamed with rhinestones. All eyes were on him when Gene said, "Now there is a troubadour if I've ever saw one, come on up fellow and sing us a song."

Del made his way to the stage. He shook Gene's hand and thanked him for bringing him up. Del said, "Kick of 'The Bottle Let Me Down' in "C"."

Gene did it just like he did on the Hag record. When the song ended, the crowd rushed the stage and filled the dance floor to capacity. Gene asked Del, "Who in hell are you anyhow?"

Del laughed and said, "Just a singer that's all."

Gene said, "Well singer, you better do another one before this bunch tears the place down." Del was kept on the stage until break.

Gene said, "Come on over to our table and let me talk to you."

When Del tried to leave the stage the fans grouped so tightly around him he had to more or less go with the flow, in this case nowhere. Fans wanted everything autographed one could imagine. One girl even proffered her ample breast for one, Del obliged. She had enough pooching out her top, that decency wasn't compromised. By the time things settled down, and he was able to get to Gene's table, it was time for the band to play again. Gene gave Del his card and said, "Come and see me."

CHAPTER 26
HOME SWEET HOME

The Fargo's arrived home to a twenty acre plot of land that Diller had groomed until it resembled a Norman Rockwell painting. Diller had, with Clark's permission and money, purchased a small diesel tractor with tiller, bush hog, and a blade. The first thing he did was bush hog the entire eighteen acres. Before grass could take it back over he tilled it all up, then turned the blade around and back bladed the entire thing. He and Ruby planted a one acre garden, and each summer harvested enough veggie's to feed them and all their friends. Diller had kept up the repairs on the two buildings, and they found things much as they left them seven years ago.

The place was a wonder to the young Aussy Tilly. She couldn't believe how different life was here compared to Sydney. She appreciated the Fargo's more then they knew, it would be almost impossible for her to be here without them. She was approved for non quota residency, due to Clark and Shelly sponsoring her. The only thing that bothered Tilly was Del Rivers wasn't here, and she cried herself to sleep each night in her longing for him.

Del Rivers was doing shows out in the southwest around Phoenix. He made enough money that he didn't have to worry about it. There were lots of women available, but Del couldn't see one without Tillie's face floating in view.

He thought, "Hell, I've got to make my way to Georgia before I go nuts." He called Clark and told him he was on the way to see them. Clark said, "Come on Del you're missed here by everyone, and I mean everyone."

That made Del feel the best he had felt since arriving back home.

Del pulled into The Fargo's drive on Saturday morning. They had a reunion right there. Del hugged Shelly, Angelina, and Cindy. He shook hands with Diller, Duke and Clark Jr. Clark introduced him to his mother Ruby. Del noticed Tilly on the porch and he went slowly over to her. The bunch went silent. Del and Tilly held each other's gaze all the time he was walking, and when he stopped, they were still lost in each other's eyes. Tilly was the first to drop her eyes. Del said, "How are you Tilly?"

YOU'RE MOVING WHERE?

Tilly couldn't find her tongue; she turned and ran inside the house. Del stood there in shock, what the heck did he do anyhow. Shelly took off at a run, as she passed him she said, "It'll be ok Del, believe me it will."

Shelly found Tilly sobbing into her pillow in her bedroom. Shelly sat down on the bed and put her hand on the girls shoulder and let her cry herself out. When Tilly calmed down to dry sobbing, Shelly asked her what the problem was.

Tilly, between sobs told her what she already knew. "She was in love with Del and she knew Del loved her too, but how could she be with Del. She belonged to the Fargo's, she couldn't possible desert them after she let them sponsor her to this beautiful country."

Shelly laughed and said, "Is that what's bothering you honey? You must know Del is like one of the family, just like you. You two need each other, and you have every right to seek happiness with anyone you want, however, we are really thrilled the one you chose to fall in love with, was our Del Rivers, and not someone we don't know."

Tilly was looking at Shelly with huge eyes. She exclaimed, "You knew? Oh Shelly, I tried to hide my feelings from you for such a long time, I'm so glad it's out now. Can I go see Del now?"

Shelly said, "You bet Tilly, let's go get him."

Tilly laughed out loud at her remark. Del was near the porch talking to Clark and his folks when Tilly ran out of the house and leaped into Del's arms.

Del had turned as the door opened, and moved towards the porch, otherwise Tilly would have busted her butt in a heap at his feet. She hung on to him and professed her love. Del told her he had fallen in love with her the very first time he saw her in Sydney. He just couldn't do anything about it then; but now he was single once more and if she would have him, would she consent to marrying him. Tilly, with no hesitation at all, said, "Yes, I will marry you."

A rebel yell went up from the Fargo bunch.

Seven days later, Del and Tilly were married in the Fargo's living room. The two took off on their honeymoon right after the ceremony. They were gone for two full weeks. By the time they returned, the two looked happy and healthy. Shelly and Clark insisted they move into Tillie's old room.

Tilly and Del made love whenever they were in the mood. Del found he loved to spend time with Tilly doing nothing more than talking. One evening Tilly told Del, "I have something to show you."

YOU'RE MOVING WHERE?

She took out a small wooden teak box from a dresser drawer. She opened the top and dumped it upside down on the bed. Del couldn't believe what he saw. The box had been full of traveler's checks of one hundred dollar denomination. "How much is it?" Del asked.

Tilly said, "Let's count it shall we?"

There were seventy six books of checks with $1000 dollars in each one. Del said, "Holy Cahones girl, where in the world did you get this much money?"

Tilly laughed, and said, "Clark has paid me 100 dollars a week for the last seven years with a yearly bonus; and I've saved all of it and the interest accumulated to this. It was in savings when we left Australia where I converted it to Travelers checks the poof is here. I've spent some of the interest for clothes and such, but I take all my meals with the Fargo's, there was no need to keep much for me self. Can we use it for anything?"

Del looked at this beautiful wife of his and said, "I'll try to do the right thing for us with it. We need to go singing before long and I think you and I ought to put a good portion of this back in savings, because it won't make any interest in its present form. We can keep some out in case we want to buy something and put the rest in cash deposits at the bank. They pay yearly interest and it will grow with time. Don't worry about money, I have saved for a few years myself, and we are financially secure."

They hugged and then made love on top of $76,000 smackeroos. She and Del would have their own private little joke about that for years.

CHAPTER 27
BACK TO MUSIC

Del heard Tilly singing one of his songs while she showered one morning, and was totally amazed. He listened until she sang all of it, and didn't hear one wrong note; he also could hear her Aussie-Scottish soft burr in every word. He was floored, and when she came out wrapped in a beach towel he took her in his arms and told her, he thought maybe she better start singing with him. Tilly said, "That has been one of me dreams ever since I met you dear. If you think I'm good enough, then I will do it."

When Del told Clark about Tillie's singing, Clark said, "You and I are two lucky dogs my good friend. I think Tilly will put us all to shame someday, you married well old son, and I'm proud of you. What do you think you're going to do next?"

Del was quiet for a bit, and then said, "When I decided to sell my park up in Alabama, I put it to vote as to where the family should go. My little daughter Pat and I voted for Alaska, but we lost out to Australia. I didn't mind, because I've always loved the mystery of Aussie land too. Well, I've seen it and the mystery is no longer there. I think I want to move up to Alaska and build a cabin in the wilderness."

"You're moving where?" Clark exclaimed.

Clark and his music bunch were devastated to lose Tilly and Del. Clark had high hopes of Del rejoining the Fargo group once again. He and his band were severely restricted without the star power of one of the best singer's he had ever heard. Del explained that Alaska was the 49th state and you could actually drive there by crossing Canada south to north. There were phones to keep in contact with and besides all that, maybe the Fargo's might want to have a visit to the last frontier sometime. This appeased Clark and Shelly and to their credit, they begin immediately to plan a trip in their minds, up the American-Canadian or Alcan Highway.

Del Rivers, through the years had accumulated six albums of cassette tapes of good quality with graphics. Some were his songs and a few were other singers' songs. People bought these by the dozen wherever he played, a simple phone call would restock his tapes.

Tilly had every one of them. She had given money to Shelly for the purchase of all the tapes

YOU'RE MOVING WHERE?

down through the years, and she knew most of the songs by heart. Del took to teaching Tilly the art of backup singing. Tilly was like a sponge, she absorbed everything Del told her, and was quick to learn. Del surprised her on her birthday with a brand new Gibson acoustic guitar. He taught her how to tune the guitar by ear, and then began showing her chords.

Tilly had extremely small hands, but she soon retrained her hands to form the chords. Rhythm was the hardest thing for her to learn. Del explained to her that every song published, had its own rhythm pattern, and this pattern was the signature of that particular song. If this wasn't done right, people wouldn't listen to the guitar picker. Tilly never worked so hard at something in her whole life. She amazed the entire bunch. She didn't always get it right, but she knew when she didn't, and worked even harder for perfection. Her backup singing was spot on, and made Del standout even more. Del told her all this until she began to believe it herself. Her self-esteem shot up sky high. She was a delight to be around to everyone, because she was so positive and upbeat, no one could be down around Tilly Rivers.

CHAPTER 28
North to Alaska

The day finally arrived for Del and Tilly to depart on their northern adventure. Shelly was in tears all morning. She felt like she was losing a daughter. Tilly had been a valued member of the Fargo family for eight years now. She would be missed a great deal by everyone. Clark Jr. and Angelina said goodbye in tears as well. Del told Clark he would keep in touch and maybe they would plan a tour at some later date that would include Alaska. Clark felt like he was saying goodbye to a brother, he told Del, anytime you want to buddy; we are your bunch too.

Del and Tilly had traded the Bedford step van for a 4x4 Chevy truck with an eleven foot slide in camper that was fully self-contained. He and Tilly bought a seventeen foot lake boat with a thirty-three horse power motor on it. They intended to fish every time they got tired of playing and singing. They had taken all the Fargo's out to the local lake and ran around

YOU'RE MOVING WHERE?

giving everyone rides. The two were proud of their handsome outfit. The truck was cream and maroon colored while the boat was sky blue and white. As the rig moved slowly out of the drive of the Fargo's house, it was the loneliest sight the Fargo's had ever seen.

Del and Tilly were sad for a few miles and then perked up. They had a whole world out there to explore, and couldn't remain in the doldrums for long. From Macon they went almost straight north at first, and then slightly west. They went through Des Moines, Iowa and didn't even slow down. The interstate went around the city. They traveled west to Rapid City, South Dakota, and then on through the north east corner of the state of Wyoming, into Montana, then on up to Sweetgrass, Montana. The Border was a small block building with the Americans at one end and the Canadians at the other. They were through and on their way to Edmonton, Alberta in a matter of minutes. The roads were single lane and went through the center of each town. The newlyweds were in no hurry and would spend time in the small town's shopping facilities. Sometimes this only consisted of a small general store with a pot bellied stove in the corner. These were their favorites. They always made fans at each stop, winding up playing and selling tapes.

Theodore Potter

They more or less left civilization behind at Edmonton, where they went mostly west by north on a highway that was either rough as a washboard or under construction. The under construction stretches were the baddies. Del was either in mud up to the hubs or negotiating rocks the size of basket balls; he really had to watch it below sheer mountain slide areas. A truck would rumble by and vibrate rocks loose that sometimes filled the roadway. Two times they had to roll huge boulders to the side in order to continue on their way. This was a dangerous thing; another rock could fall at any moment. The road stretched out forever in front of them. There was so much mud on the boat and truck Del couldn't tell what color they were. When they reached Watson Lake, British Colombia, Tilly saw a car wash and excitedly pointed it out to Del. They pulled in and put on old clothes, and with a great deal of work and forty dollars' worth of Canadian quarters, they removed an inch of black caked on baked on mud from the truck and boat. The truck and boat being new came up pretty good, but would need to be detailed when they reached Fairbanks.

Del and Tilly were thrilled by all the wild country they had seen for the past two weeks, but it sure was good to see the border and customs of Alaska. They were asked if they were

YOU'RE MOVING WHERE?

American Citizens, and did they have anything to declare? Del saw no reason to complicate things so he said yes, and no they didn't have anything to declare. They drove down the hill on paved roads, into the interior of the last frontier.

CHAPTER 29
ALASKA!

The first town they came to was Northway, some forty miles into Alaska. It was no more than a small store and a gas pump. Del filled up the two tanks on the truck and talked to the store owner. He was an old Sourdough, and had lived here for the last thirty-five years and was convinced things were going straight to hell in a hand basket. What with the road getting fixed and all more Cheechokos, naive newcomers to Alaska, than a man could contend with would be coming up it and before long a man wouldn't have room to spit. He had a grin on his face as he talked rapid fire.

Del and Tilly didn't get a word in until they said so long to the most talkative person they had met on their trip.

Tok, the second town in Alaska was a neat wide spot in the road that sported 600 souls during summer and dwindled to a mere 250 in the bitter winters. There was a grocery store and

YOU'RE MOVING WHERE?

two bars. The road went straight on to Fairbanks, and the cut off went left to Glenallen, Palmer, and on to Anchorage, a city with a population of 250,000 winter residents that would swell to 300,000 in the summer. Del and Tilly continued on to Fairbanks.

There was twenty four hours of daylight on the twenty-second of June 1980 when the two singers arrived in Fairbanks, Alaska. First, they cleaned the boat, truck, and camper up. This took hours of work. They were worn out both from the trip and hard work of removing 5,000 miles of grime and dirt. They checked into the Norlite camp ground just off Airport way, off Peger road and swore they wouldn't move for a week.

The only more grueling trip Del remembered was the road from Goldworthy Mine to Broom, Western Australia. None of it was meant for anything but huge ore hauling machines. Some of the Alcan was pretty good and improving each year. Del and Tilly were made aware of the fact that a late fall trip is much more pleasant, and much easier on machine and man. They learned a lot just talking to folks around the campground and town. Del was irked at some of the cheechocko's that had landed in Alaska a week or so before he and Tilly, thinking it made them experts on all aspects of life in Alaska, and voicing their opinion loud and long. Del learned real quick to ask them, "How long did you say you've been in Alaska?"

This cut down on wasted time, even if it did cause a few red faces. The owner of the camp ground heard Del and Tilly play and sing, and became a fan instantly. She also was a wealth of information. Mary had three children age seven through eleven, and they become fans of the two as well. Mary told Tilly they should do good out on the rivers of Alaska.

Each Village along the Yukon River had a community gathering place, and if Tilly and Del could somehow travel on the river system in a live aboard boat of some type, they would sell many tapes. Del had thought about doing just that. He was part Indian and could negotiate with the Athabascan Indians that inhabited those Villages.

Del and Tilly went boat shopping. Del was going to try and find a boat he and Tilly could live comfortable on and navigate a river he knew nothing about. Del was fairly acquainted with boats. His first experience was a nineteen foot plywood cabin cruiser he rebuilt and powered with a used seventy-five horsepower outboard that left him stranded out of sight of land in the Gulf of Mexico. Then the damn thing lost a sheet of fiber glass off its bottom on a lake in Alabama,

YOU'RE MOVING WHERE?

and sank not thirty feet from the shore. He and his four kids had to swim. Del liked to never have lived that one down, and his wife Dedi, never missed a chance to remind him of it. Del wanted no repeat of that. He told Tilly they would only buy something that was solid wood or fiberglass.

The only place in Fairbanks with big boats for sale was Smarts Marina down on Front Street, across the Chena River from Fairbanks proper. They went walking through all the boats looking, when this fellow came over to them and ask if he could help them. He could tell these two were as green as they could possibly be. Del told him what they were looking for. He was silent for a couple of seconds, and then he spoke, "Well, we don't have many choice's here in Fairbanks, but I'll show what we have."

He walked to a boat he said was made of teak and cypress. It was a pretty thing. Tilly cooed and awed at it. Del was looking at the motor and the way it was mounted. It was a Honda 85 horse and was mounted on a lift mechanism that raised the motor up out of the water. The guy said, "You're looking at a lower end saver that allows you to run in one foot of water, and is electrically operated by a switch in the cockpit."

Del was impressed and began to look the rest of the boat over. It was an eighteen foot flat bottom, and had a beautiful cabin with two bunks and a small galley, with an alcohol cook stove. There was a head tucked in the corner at the end of the bunk beds. Del passed through the forward hatch to the bow. The hatch slid to the rear, and the door opened in and was also the head door. The cockpit was in the right front of the cabin, making it possible for the skipper to stand in the hatch way and steer the boat. Del's mind was made up, he said, "How much?"

The guy smiled and said, "You had better set down sir, before I tell you."

He added, "The price is $37,510 with no tax."

Del asked, "How much will you allow for the boat I'm towing?"

The guy walked around the 17 foot Boston whaler, and took a boat book out and did some calculations. He said, "Your boat is almost new, so I'll allow you $9500 as trade in."

Del didn't even hesitate, he said, "I'll write you a check right now, and when it clears you call and I'll pick her up. I'll let you keep the trade-in here. We're down at the Norlite campground, and you can call Mary there, and tell her when we can come and pick her up."

The guy thought, "That'll teach me to not pre judge people".

YOU'RE MOVING WHERE?

Del and Tilly went shopping for stuff they would need out on the river. They spent most of the day buying everything from bug dope, to dry egg mix and rain gear. The camper was noticeably lower in the ass end on the return trip to the campground. As they pulled in to Norlite, the oldest curly red haired daughter of Mary came bounding out to meet them. Del stopped and she jumped on the running board and told them the new boat was ready to be picked up. Del and Tilly really liked this family. They thanked her and drove on, after she dropped off the running board.

When they towed the boat down to their camp site it caused quite a stir among a camp ground filled to capacity with Chechocko's. By the time they arrived at their site, they had an audience of curious on lookers that were also fans. Del had to explain to them about the boat and its inner workings and what they were going to do with it. Finally the people went home and left them alone.

Tilly worked her buns off packing things from the camper into the boat. Del went to talk to Mary about storing the pickup and camper here with them. As he walked through the camp ground he noticed every rock in the park had a different scene painted on it. Someone was quite the Artist. He asked Mary about the rocks, and

Mary said, "Yes, my daughter paint's anything that doesn't move, so don't stop too long here or you will have a painting on you Del."

They both laughed at that. Del had a sudden inspiration. The boat needed a name painted on it. He asked Mary if the girl might be interested in painting a name on the boat for him. Mary yelled through a door, which must lead to living quarters, "Dasey come out here please, someone needs to talk to you".

The girl came bouncing out and when she saw who it was she instantly become shy. Del said, "I've been admiring your paintings about the park. You are a good little artist."

She raised her head and said, "I'm not that little, and I'll be twelve in one month."

Mary and Del knew a crush when they saw it. Del said, "Well you are a big girl at that. I need you to do some painting on my new boat. Will you do it for me?"

She said, "Yes if I can I will."

Del said, "You will have to do it while I keep my wife away, because it's her name you'll be painting on the boat, and I want to surprise her."

Dasey clapped her hands and said, "Oh I love surprises, when can I do it?"

Del said, "Tomorrow morning. We'll go shopping and you can do it while were gone."

YOU'RE MOVING WHERE?

Del drew a pitiful drawing of the boat, and put TILLY on each side of the bow and across the stern. He wrote 4 inch letters on the bow and 8 inch on the stern. Dasey said, "I can do that with no problem."

She had calf eyes that followed Del's every move. This little gal was going to break some hearts before she was through with life. Del was used to it, he had had too many young girls getting crushes on him in his life and it was embarrassing, to say the least.

Del and Tilly made their final shopping trip last through lunch. They stopped at Pikes Landing to eat, and then went on to the camp ground. The girl had done a beautiful job of painting TILLY on the boat. Tilly didn't notice at first.

It was an hour later that she did notice. She let out a yell that defied her size and came running to Del and jumped in his arms and said, "You are the most wonderful man in the world do you know that?"

Del had a huge grin on his face. He felt good about things. He had done something right. His first wife Dedi would have had something derogatory to say about something like this. Tilly was tearing down the fences Del had put up around his heart to protect it from the bitter woman's tongue lashings, endured for 15 years.

It was time to hit the trail or River in this case. He and Tilly had worked like beavers to get things ready, and still he knew they would probably forget things. The fifty gallon of gas was the most difficult thing to get aboard the boat after they launched her. Del pulled the Tilly alongside the bank and moored her at bow and stern. They found some planks on the bank of the Chena that allowed them to roll the drum of gasoline on to the gunnels and tip it down into the boat. One slip and there wouldn't be a bottom in the Tilly.

They left their pickup and camper with Mary, Del had arranged it when he hired Dasey to paint the Tilly. He told her how good of a job she did on the boat. Del asked her how much he owed her she said, "I can't charge you Mr. Rivers. I was happy to do it."

Del pulled two twenties out and handed them to the girl and said, "You deserve to be paid and don't back talk me about it."

He winked at Mary and said, "See you in the fall. How about calling me a cab?"

Mary with a smile said, "OK so you're a cab, now. Why don't I give you and Tilly a ride down to your boat."

Del eased the Tilly out into the Chena and accelerated. The 85 Honda was a sweet engine. The boat went on step at just above half throttle.

YOU'RE MOVING WHERE?

She ran straight and level and responded to the wheel with ease, she was worth every cent they had paid for her.

CHAPTER 30
MUSIC ON THE RIVER

The Chena dumps into the dirty mess of water named the Tananna River just a couple of miles from Fairbanks. Tilly said, "YUK".

Del said, "What a revolting development. We don't want that crud going through our engine anymore then we have to, we will float and use the silent engine as a rudder all the way to the Yukon, where the water will clean up some I reckon."

It was pleasant floating down the river. There wasn't any wind to speak of, so it was hot and the two stripped down to bare essentials and got a tan and made love and tanned for two hours and made love again.

The next day the Nenana Silver Bridge across the Tanana River on the parks hi way hove into view. Tilly got real excited, and jumped up and down. Del was nonplused. He had no idea they could have begun their trip here

YOU'RE MOVING WHERE?

instead of Fairbanks. Del told Tilly not to look for anymore bridges from here on out. They pulled in to the dock at Nenana and went for a walk around town. There wasn't much to see and they were on their way in a few minutes. It was late in the evening and the only thing open was the bar.

Del had to learn to navigate the River from scratch. There were plenty of pitfalls at every bend they came to. The worst one of course was shallow water over rocks. This could tear the bottom out of the Tilly. Del had one experience with a reef the boat had drifted onto. He then stopped and studied the shore line and noticed when there was an outcrop of land, it in all probability extended into the water out of sight. He quickly become an expert on the River, and never hit a reef again. He simply ran a zigzag course around the reefs.

The Tilly was a wonder. It began to pour rain on their fifth day and they thought it would never stop. Del decided not to run in the heavy rain and parked the Tilly in a cove that he later learned was called an Eddie. The water did a circle and came back into itself. It was raining so hard that the bugs were grounded. Del tied the bow line to a tree and they went to sleep.

Something woke Del up and he sat up on his bunk. Tilly was still sound asleep. He eased back to the rear hatch and slid it forward. When he stuck his head out, he was near crapping himself. The cove was filled to capacity with driftwood and was in the process of pushing the Tilly crookedly up out of the water. They were high and dry, and entrapped by tons of driftwood. Del thought there ought to be a song in this deal. He yelled at Tilly to get up, they had a crisis in full swing.

After they dressed Del told Tilly, "We need to float some of this driftwood out of the cove, and let it go down river. That will free us up."

It had stopped raining, but the river was rising with flooding from all the streams dumping in it up river.

Del tested the depth of the water and found it was no more than four feet deep. He had put his hip waders on and began to pull the log jam apart. He could feel the bitter cold of the river through the thin fabric of his waders. After three hours of back breaking work up to his waist in ice cold water, the Tilly finally sat back down in the water. Del got aboard and fired her up and took her out into the flood. He had to look out for huge uprooted trees that floated along with them. The trees rolled over and over and had huge root systems on them that could crush the Tilly and them along with it. Del was glad to see the Yukon come in sight. The little Village of Tanana snuggled in the crook of land where the

YOU'RE MOVING WHERE?

Tanana and Yukon joined into one. This was to be their first stop to play music. They tied the Tilly up below the Village on the beach where many trees washed up they could secure the line to.

Word travels fast though the Alaskan bush. The people of Tanana already knew the two singers were on their way, and were met on the beach by the village elders and a covey of young Indians. Hands were shook and everyone sat on the beach and discussed what would happen. The head elder, a man of 65-70 years said, "We can't have any alcohol in Village. You must not bring it in either."

Del told him they didn't have any on board. The Elder said, "You may play tonight from seven pm till whenever,"

He got up and left without another word. Some of the young boys and girls stayed and talked to the two singers. Del ask them if the Tilly was safe to leave alone while they sang tonight, A look was exchanged between the Indians, and one of them said, "We will make sure it's not bothered."

The Concert went off without a hitch, and they sold almost twenty-five or so tapes. Everyone that bought tapes bought all eight of them. Del gave some away to the little ones who didn't have money. One small child stood there with big crock tears coursing down her cheeks. Tilly scooped her up in her arms and asked what the matter was. Between sobs the child told her she didn't have money for a tape. Tilly took her over to the table of tapes and told her to pick one. Del and Tilly exchanged looks and Del gave her thumbs up. They could afford it.

Next they came to a town shown on the map as Kockrines. It was about two days float from Tanana on the north bank of the river in a long valley. There were only two cabins in the place. As they floated by, two bearded old men came as fast as old men can move down to the bank and walked along with them. One with a Scottish accent said, "Now where ye be goin in sech a roosh?"

Tilly heard the man's accent and threw him the bow line. He made it fast to a tree root, and sat down on the tree panting like a hound pup. He said, "I be Shane Mc Glennock und I be here in this country by the grace of not being caught yet and shipped back to me homeland, and this be me fishing and trapping parrtner Joseph Longtree froom Doun riverr."

Del was fascinated by the old man and his brogue. Each word that had an R in it he rolled around his tongue and the resulting sound was pleasant to his and Tilly's ears. Tilly answered his introductions by introducing the two of them.

YOU'RE MOVING WHERE?

Del noticed Tilly's accent deepened considerably when she talked to Shane. He enjoyed listening to them talk.

They spent three days there and made good friends of Shane and Joseph. They had to promise the two sourdoughs they would stop by on their way back up River and visit longer. Tilly was in tears when they pulled out. Del understood; this girl had no relatives that she knew of, and she cared for old Shane like a grandfather and they would want to visit the Kockrines hot springs once more.

The first time they jumped in they couldn't stand the high temperature for long before it felt like their flesh would melt off their bodies. Del discovered a cold water stream dumping into the south end of the pool. If they were where the hot and cold water mixed, they had a wonderful bath. That alone was reason to visit the two endearing old sourdoughs again.

The ride down to Ruby was for the most part a peaceful ten hour trip. Del wanted to gas up there if at all possible. The two tanks on the Tilly were down to a quarter. They still had the full drum of gas as spare, but didn't want to use it if it wasn't necessary. As they pulled into the beach below the big fuel tanks mounted high upon the bank of the Yukon, there was some young Indians sitting in front of what probably was the office. It was no more than a shack, and could use a paint job. Del and Tilly walked up to the fellow's and said, "Hello, we're Del and Tilly and we would like to buy some gas for our boat."

The three was silent for a moment, and then one of them said, "You will have to go see our boss, John P Hony, and ask him, and if he say ok we sell you some gas."

The other two youths rolled their eyes as if to say, what a load of crap. Del said, "Well, tell me where I can find this P Hony."

They all pointed to a building by itself on the next level of the town, which consisted of a collection of log cabins, and a few kit houses.

When they knocked on the city hall door, nothing happened. Del was about to push the door open, when a voice from their rear asked loudly, "What do you want here in our town?"

Del turned slowly around and was confronted with a short surly Indian of forty years or so. Tilly, trying to circumvent a clash between the two men, said in her broadest Scottish Brogue; "Ai we arri in need oof petrol fer ourr boot. Can youu selle oos a bit o gas me goot Mon."

Del came near to pissing himself from the way John P Hony looked at Tilly, who was rolling her beautiful blue eyes at him, his lower jaw was down near his scrotum by this time. Del had to

YOU'RE MOVING WHERE?

walk away, he was near to cracking up, and if he did, he knew Hony, who obviously didn't care a whiff about white folk anyhow, would never sell them gas. He walked back to the boat, it was best to let his talented wife handle this Indian.

Tilly walked down a few minutes later with a smug look on her face, and said, "We are allowed to fill up." She cracked up along with Del.

There was nothing else to do. The three young men looked at Tilly in amazement. Hony had called down and said, "Let them have as much as they need."

This had never happened before. Gasoline was a hard commodity to come by out here on the River and usually, he let people have only enough to reach the next town. In this case being Galena, down river fifty-six miles. The guys jumped to the refueling of the boat like never before. The job was finished in no time flat.

The three asked Del and Tilly if they were going to play some music for the Village. Del said, "Yes they would play at seven pm, right here at the boat."

Two of the young men took off at a run to inform the Village folks there was to be a free concert on the beach this evening.

Their next stop was Galena where there was an Air Force base, and there was a population of 600. They were mostly Indians with only a few white folk. There weren't enough bodies on the air base to have a show there, so they did one at Hobo Benson's open bar. A good crowd came out and Del and Tilly responded with a good show.

Del and Hobo become good friends after the concert. He told Del he and his beautiful wife shouldn't go any farther down river. Over the years some folk failed to pay attention, and were never heard from again. Someone would come to Glena, asking if anyone had seen their Dad, Mother, Sister or Brother. Hobo said, "The River doesn't give up its dead easily."

Del and Tilly talked it over and agreed with Hobo. They would move back up the river when they were tired of Galena. Del caught some young kid trying to steal gas out of his full drum on the boat. He collard the boy and took him up to Hobo. There was an Alaska State Trooper stationed in Galena, but Del didn't want to see this kid ruin his life over a bit of gas. Hobo, on the other hand simply said, "Call the police and teach the little s--t a lesson."

At this the little s--t turned into a little boy and told Del he was sorry. He would do anything for Del and Tilly, please don't call Trooper. Hobo averted his head and smiled. He had dealt with these people for many years, and knew how to use reverse psychology on them to bring them in line. Hobo asked Del, "What sort of work do you have for this lad to do?"

Del was silent for a spell, and then he said, "I think I need a boat guard don't you think so Hobo?"

He could see Hobo Benson's shoulders shaking with mirth. Del asked the boy if that would be ok. The boy knew he had been hornswaggled. He just didn't know any way out of the revolting situation. To the boy's credit he took the safety of the Tilly to heart, and told all the others they didn't want to mess with the big guy's boat. Hobo explained to Del that he had done more good then he knew. The Indians out here wouldn't steal from a friend and he had just made the kid one. "Mind you they may still attempt to borrow from a friend and have every intention of returning the item, and sometimes they really did." laughed Hobo."

CHAPTER 31
TRIP UP RIVER

Del and Tilly bypassed Ruby and boated all the way to Kockrines and their two old friends Shane and Joe. The two were really happy to see them and they were determined to keep the two here for a spell. Shane led them over to a spare cabin and told them they might want to move in it for a while. There was a pleading look in the old guy's eyes and it hurt Del to have to tell them the boat was their home out here on the river.

He didn't tell them how bad the cabin smelled in the warm, end of July weather. Del promised them he and Tilly would stay as long as possible. They had to beat the ice getting to Fairbanks, because they didn't want to stay out all winter. Shane said, "That will be the end of August ye moust leave here by then."

Del asked them when they normally received the first frost out here. Both old men got a little

YOU'RE MOVING WHERE?

red in the face, and Joe said, "Normally about the fifteenth of August."

Del said, "Well, we can stay until the seventh of August and that's ten days from now."

Del and Tilly had a bath in the hot/cold spring each day, and explored Kockrines. Joe told them stories about the town and its faded glory days of gold mining.

Tilly wanted to know why no one else lived in the town site. Joe said, "Back when the town was full of miners some young Indian bucks had drank whisky and broke into the Catholic Church and desecrated the alter by taking a dump on it. As you might guess, this shameful act thoroughly cheesed the priest off and he called a town meeting of all people. When they were assembled, the angry priest declared that grass would grow on the streets of Kockrines. Well the Indians being a superstitious lot, stopped walking on the streets, and sure enough the priest's prophesy came true. The Indians moved in mass down river to Ruby and then gold was discovered there, and all the miners deserted the town as well."

Old Joe was laughing by the time he finished the story.

The seventh of August arrived too soon for the four friends. Del and Tilly both had a hard time leaving because they knew they would never see them again. Finally they were on their way. Tilly was openly crying her eyes out, and Del even felt choked up as the Tilly moved out of sight of the still waving old sourdoughs.

CHAPTER 32
GEORGIA CALLING

The trip up river had been arduous for the two humans and hard on the boat. Del and Tilly had to make many temporary repairs to the Tilly, primarily to the prop and engine. No matter how hard Del tried, he hit things under water that shouldn't be there. He had to redress the prop three times before finally reaching the calm Chena River near Fairbanks Alaska. It was the fifteenth of August when they pulled the Tilly out of the water at the University crossing. Del looked the bottom end of the big Hondo outboard over, and told Tilly they were lucky to have made it. He vowed to never do it again without a spare bottom end for it.

Mary and her children were happy to see them and promptly threw a barbecue in honor of Del and Tilly. Mary's husband was home from Prudhoe Bay up on the North Slope. He worked 200 days out of the year helping to extract oil out of the ground and shipping it via the Trans-

Alaska Pipe Line to Valdez down on the south central coast. His name was Ernest, and he was friendly and open like Mary.

The barbecue was a great success, half of Fairbanks showed up, or least it seemed like, to the two singers. Their popularity had spread back up the river, and the people wanted more of Del and Tilly than they had time to give.

On the eighteenth of August, Del promised Mary to keep in touch and he and Tilly packed up and headed down the Alcan Highway. The trip back to Georgia would be a long one.

CHAPTER 33
BACK IN GEORGIA

Clark looked at what he and his son and dad had done and was proud of all three of them. They had ten acres of different crops they were harvesting. The fresh veggie stand, out on the 134 was doing business like crazy. Shelly and Angelia were having the time of their life selling the produce he and his dad and son produced. Clark and the bunch did music on the weekends while Diller and Ruby ran the roadside stand.

Shelly picked up the phone when it rang and jumped to her feet letting go a rebel whoop that was heard out on the porch where Clark, Brad, Doc and Duke were sipping sweet tea from frosty glasses. Clark went in to see what had stirred his wife up. She said, "It's Del and Tilly, they're on their way down and will be here tomorrow."

There was great excitement at the Fargo Ranch. Tilly was coming home, dragging Del with her. When the two pulled into the yard,

Shelly ran to the passenger side and when the door was flung open, she and Tilly engulfed each other in arms. Both were crying tears of happiness. Clark Sr and Jr shook Del's hand and Angelia hugged Del, and thanked him for bringing Tilly home.

CHAPTER 34
PUTTING THE SHOW BACK TOGETHER

Clark and Del put their heads together and mapped out a plan of action for the Fargo's along with Del and Tilly. Del reasoned that Clark had one of the best country bands around and that was their ace in the hole. Del told him he thought they should recruit someone to play bass guitar for the bunch. That would turn Clark loose to MC and not have to play the entire three hour show. Clark thought that was a damn good idea, and told Del he could put his hands on any number of bass players, but they should walk softly in their selection.

The Show made its debut, at the Holiday Inn on the bypass on a Saturday night. There were 350 folks there to see all their mistakes.

The main problem was Tillie's lack of stage experience before a large audience. Tilly bless her heart, pulled her boot straps up in the last half of the show, and left the stage with a high volume of applause for her efforts.

Unknown to Del, Clark had invited his TV show producer Rick, out to review the show. At the end the bunch had to do two curtain calls. Rick came back stage and shook Clark's hand. Clark introduced Rick to Del. Rick said, "You impressed me a great deal Del. I think you are star quality and I'm prepared to help you and this bunch obtain that status. Come around to the office at the station tomorrow and we will discuss it."

Rick went around and shook all the guys and girls hands. He knew he was in the presence of future greatness with this bunch. He would be their friend from now on.

As for the show, it was such a success; folks were buying tapes of Del's and Clark's music left and right. The two co-stars sat on the stage steps signing each tape J card with their autograph. The manager hovered around, ushering people to the tape and photo table and then back to where Del and Clark was signing the records and Photo's. He had become a great fan and wanted to book the show again right away. Clark explained they would get back to him in a few days on that. The manager was a bit miffed, but got over it real quick; he was

YOU'RE MOVING WHERE?

enjoying the bunch too much to stay mad at them.

Rick was turning out to be just what the group needed. Management. He said, "I need a change in my job and if you two will have me I will put you where you belong. I've already been in contact with my good friend Robert Hensley up in Tulsa, and he informed me, if I said you had star quality that was good enough for him. You are booked in to the Tulsa pavilion on the fifteenth of next month. That gives us over a month to promote the thing and fill 30,000 seats."

"It will take all of our combined efforts to do that. I have the studio and own the better part of it. You boys need to spend about a week putting down whatever you have written since you recorded last. The studio and an engineer are at your disposal 24/7."

Del stood and shook Rick's hand and said, "I think I speak for everyone Rick, welcome to the bunch."

Clark jumped up and said, "Hear, hear".

CHAPTER 35
THE BIG TIME

It was a bit disconcerting to gaze out over the waves of bodies that had bought tickets to see the Fargo bunch. Del Rivers was the only one who had played to anything close to this; it was at the Tumbarumba Rodeo down in the Snowy Mountains, in southern New South Wales, over in Australia. The big difference was, these folks bought tickets to see them, and the rodeo folks bought them to see cows and horses. He supposed they were one step up the ladder now.

It had been fun work promoting themselves for the last five weeks. Radio talk show after talk show had resulted in a lot of record and tape sales and caused a terrific increase in the Show's popularity, in the mid-west portion of the country. The show had played the Cain's Ball Room in Tulsa Oklahoma, to standing room only, and made a bunch of new fans. Robert Hensley came to that show at Cain's, and after the show visited with all the members. He singled Tilly out and took both her hands in his and stated, "You, my fine young lady, are the brightest light I've seen in a long time." He continued, "All in the show are stars in their own right, but you my dear, are destined to become a superstar."

Tilly grew red in the face and thanked Robert, she said, "I only want to sing and please the people Mr. Hensley."

Robert countered with, "And that my dear is why you will be a superstar."

Del was so proud of Tilly he was near busting. He knew when Tilly had sung her solo tonight, and brought the house down, he was a lucky man. He could move into managing his beautiful wife with pride. He was tired; too many appearances across too many years had dulled his cutting edge as a performer. Sometimes he was surprised when he made it one more time.

The curtain rose on the Fargo bunch and they put on a fantastic show. Del Introduced Tilly and a hush fell on the crowd. Tilly sang her song in her soft Scottish burr, and laid nerves bare in 90% of the people. She put more drive in the song as it progressed and had 100% on their feet for the last minute of the song. The band was applauding with the audience, and had to do another verse and chorus. It was a good thing the half way break was next and the curtain fell.

In order to appease the audience Del took a remote mic out front of the curtain to talk to the fans. In his best golden voice he explained that Tilly would be out in the second half and would do more than one song. He said, "You have shown us, that what we suspected is without a doubt true. Tilly would soon be the star of her own show."

This caused a great roar from the huge crowd. Tilly was concerned she might've done something wrong. Del hugged her and told her she was just the best thing that had happened to the show. He told her to think of five songs to do in the second half. Tilly smiled and said it wasn't any problem; she had fifty or so to choose from not counting the ones he had wrote for her.

Tilly chose "Say-Ya-Do", a bouncy tune Del wrote for her about the time they first got together. The crowd went absolutely nuts and wouldn't stop raising hell until she sang it one more time. Tilly had her first hit. Rick sitting in the audience was dumb struck by the fans reaction to Tilly's singing. Tilly went right in to another song Del wrote called, "You Cheated and Lied". There was no mistake; this girl had what it takes to be a superstar. Rick thought he must get her in the studio here in Tulsa tomorrow. The fans made her do half of the song over again, and when she came to the line, 'but

YOU'RE MOVING WHERE?

dang it all, I came back for more', the crowd erupted with such a roar it was scary. Tilly let the roar subside, and then said, "You are the most wonderful audience I have ever known, I want to do another song my husband Del Rivers wrote. I need your help on this one though. You need to sing "please walk back to me", each time I sing it to you."

Tilly took off on the song called "Please Walk Back", and before her and the audience were through they had it down perfect. Rick wished then he had known about Tilly before, if he had he would have had a mobile recording unit here. Well, he vowed, no more chances were going to slip by this old boy, he had the real deal here and by damn he was going to do the job he hired on to do.

CHAPTER 35
A NEW STAR IN BORN

Rick collard Del after the show and told him, "Breakfast is on me, ten am in the restaurant of the Holiday Inn. Bring Tilly please."

Del knew Rick was up to doing well and he had a pretty good idea what it pertained to. Tilly, that's who and Del, knew Rick was right. His wonderful wife was on her way to the top. All he would do was direct traffic and protect his wife. Tilly had a great head on her shoulders and could be a little stubborn from time to time, but if given a chance to think things out, she always made the proper choice.

What a turn of events. Tilly's first recording "You Cheated And Lied', went straight to number one like a bullet. "Say-Ya-Do" run a close second but topped out at three. Del told Rick why. You followed the other song too close. Give these songs a chance to breathe and you will have a string of number one hits, and when the full album is released we will have a number one hit there too. Rick couldn't help but think; this old boy knows what the hell he's talking about.

Tilly did become a superstar, however not by that name and you watch her make hits right to present day.

CHAPTER 36
GROWING OLD GRACEFULLY

Clark and Shelly were in tears. Their little girl Angelina was no longer little. She was all grown up and getting married to one of the nicest guys in Georgia. David Robert Glenover had walked into their little girl's life at the big mall where her Grandmother's house had stood for fifty-seven years. The courtship had been sometimes comical and sometimes heartbreaking. When David first attempted to "get to know the parents" he knocked on the door and Clark of all people answered it. He beheld a strange sight. The kid was a geeky looking seventeen year old. His hair was plastered to his head by some kind of oil and tufts of it protruded from a long billed hat with only a band and a bill. His pants were too short and his argyle socks were visible clean up to the elastic around the top. His shoes were black and white tennis shoes and were scuffed all over. Before the kid could get a word out, Clark got tickled and not being able to help

YOU'RE MOVING WHERE?

himself, doubled over with mirth. The kid's face grew red with embarrassment as he shifted from one foot to the other.

The boy then began to lose his temper. He said, "I'm David Glenover and I am a friend of your daughter Angelina, may I talk to her please?"

Clark stopped laughing and turned serious. He sternly asked, "Just where in the hell do you know my daughter from?"

Scared out of his wits, David squeaked, "From the mall."

Clark said, "Come in and sit down and I will ask my daughter if she wants to see you, although I can't imagine why she would want to."

Clark was trying to hide his laughter, but it was hard. He walked down the hall and there was his daughter and wife Shelly. Shelly commented, "Kinda hard on the kid weren't you big guy?"

She and Clark grinned at each other. Angelina looked at her dad with daggers, but said. "He really is a nice person dad, don't be so difficult."

Then she hugged him. Now they were becoming man and wife four years later. The relationship had been a rocky one with more ups and downs than Shelly and Clark could keep up with. The past year had seen the two settle down and start to think about the future. Finally the two came to Clark and Shelly and sorted out their future together. David had a killer job in computers; making their future financially secure. Shelly told them the main reason for marriage failure was lack of money. Clark told the two he and Shelly would see they had a nest egg to build on.

Clark was a man of his word and as soon as the two returned from their Honeymoon he would deposit $50.000 in an account for them. If the boy was smart enough he would parlay that into a fortune, if not he would help them again and again, because they were a family and he had the means.

The wedding was in the planning stage so long, that Clark had to get away for a spell. As luck would have it Del and Tilly flew in for the wedding from Tok, Alaska. Del and Clark said, "The hell with it," and went fishing out on the lake. It was late May and the crappie was spawning and as long as you could keep a live minnow on the hook you would pull one in. They took fifty pounds of cleaned and iced filet's home in a cooler. There would be one big fish fry this weekend.

Shelly and Tilly spent hours catching up. Tilly spent 200 days on the road each year doing concerts while Del had a small band he played a

YOU'RE MOVING WHERE?

limited number of concerts with from time to time, he wanted no more than that. He met Tilly and her gang for 100 shows a year and that took most of his time. Del told Clark he should come with him and goof around a bit doing music. Clark and Fargo were still playing from time to time around the country but if he could see his way clear, he would do that.

The wedding day arrived and over 100 invited guests flocked to the Fargo mini farm. Clark had built a huge covered stage and barbeque area and the wedding was to be held there. The best man was a fellow about David's age. He stayed as far from Clark as possible. David had some fun and told him, "Clark is one bad dude, stay away from him."

Once during the day Clark found himself face to face with this kid, and the boy, with a fearful look in his eyes bolted for safety. Clark saw David cracking up. He walked over to his soon to be son-in-law and asked him, "What in the hell did you tell your best man?"

David said with a poker face, "The truth that's all sir."

Clark cuffed him playfully up beside the head. "You told him some bull about me didn't you?"

He stated. David said, "Well, paybacks are sweet aren't they?"

The boy moved away fast to prevent what he knew wouldn't be no love tap this time. He sprinted away at a speed that caused Fargo to mutter, "Ah to be young once again."

He was still laughing when Shelly found him and latched on to him. She said, "The wedding is about to start."

He saw his mom and dad near the shed as they called it, and it hit him suddenly how old and frail they had become without him realizing it. Heck he was forty-four and on the downhill run. But he didn't feel it and that's what mattered.

CHAPTER 37
BACK IN THE GAME

Del and Tilly Rivers enjoyed the wedding and the reception afterwards. When the entire mess of guest was gone and the happy couple dispatched on their honeymoon, they set on the front porch and talked with the Fargo's. Clark said, "You know I just realized today, time is slipping away on us, were you serious about us doing some music together again Del?"

Del said, "Well, hell yes I was man."

Clark said, "I would have to take my band boys with me."

Del said, "The guys I play with are too old and set in their ways to travel, so that'll work out."

Tilly piped up with, "You can open for me for 200 shows a year."

The silence was like electricity, it crackled. Then everyone tried to talk at once. Del said, "Whoa folks, why didn't I think of that."

Tilly asked if they wanted her to arrange it. Clark and Del spoke in unison- "Yes!" Tilly spent an hour on the phone and came outside all smiles. "It looks like you guys are doing 200 shows a year with me."

Del and Clark shook their heads in wonder. Both had thoughts of this wonderful girl driving them around Sydney Australia so long ago in a rental car. Now she was in essence becoming their boss. Boy howdy.

CHAPTER 38
HOW SWEET IT IS

The long bus pulled into the Gaylord Entertainment Complex at Opryland in Nashville, Tennessee. The driver was none other than Gene Cornwell from Des Moines, Iowa. He was a close friend to Del and Tilly; the two had met him in Corpus Christy, Texas on the beach. Del and Tilly had parked their camper van on the National seashore and spent time between shows there. They both loved the sound of the surf and the salty air. One morning as Del set outside of the camper, he noticed a tall fellow knocking golf balls into the surf. Del had a ball he found and thought he would take it to him. He never thought such a great friendship would spawn from such a simple act.

Del and Tilly stayed in contact with Gene and when they needed a driver he was ecstatic to have the job. He loved music and had a golden pass to every concert they performed, and got paid as well. Tonight he had to be content with the DVD machine on the bus. The Opry was booked solid and Tilly was just a guest on the show. Only musicians and singers got to go. This was the first for Fargo. Del had been with Tilly the two times she appeared before. They were picking and singing back stage, but no one asked Del to play on stage. Tilly was a different story. Word was out she was to be asked to join the Opry.

Brad Paisley came on microphone and said "Ladies and gentleman; we have a treat for you tonight. We have a wonderful Aussie singer making her third appearance on the Opry tonight and you'll love her singing. I'm talking about the one and only Miss Tilly Rivers. Make her welcome."

The applause was thundering as Tilly skipped out on stage with a brilliant smile in place. When the huge audience settled down, Tilly sang "You Cheated And Lied". The crowd swayed from side to side throughout the song, and when it was finished they came to their feet once more. Tilly sang one more called "Whisky Greed And The Devil Had Control". Brad came out at the end and held onto Tilly who was ready to bolt for the wings. Brad said, "We have a surprise for you Tilly. This is your third appearance on this stage and you have become precious to us and your fans. We want to

YOU'RE MOVING WHERE?

welcome one of the longest performing members of the grand ole Opry to present to you, something we hope you accept. Ladies and gentleman welcome my friend, Little Jimmy Dickens!"

Short Jimmy came out and stood on the milk box he always stood on. He was still shorter then Tilly. He said, "I take pleasure in informing you Miss Tilly, that you have been inducted as a member of the Grand Ole Opry."

The crowd went wild and it was hopeless for a good bit. When the fans settled down, Tilly took the microphone off the stand and walked to the front edge of the stage where she could see the faces in the audience. She said softly in her pronounced Scottish brogue. "I dinou get here all by me self. Along time ago, a man believed in me and taught me to sing and play the guitar. He wrote the two songs I sing for you tonight and has been the best friend and husband this Girl could hope for. Please welcome my husband, Del Rivers out for a bow."

Del walked on stage to thundering applause, He hugged Tilly and whispered in her ear, you did it Babe, congratulations. He and Tilly walked off stage to a standing ovation. Back stage there were hugs and handshakes all around. Brad and Jimmy Dickens came over to Del and shook his hand. Tilly and Del were the chosen ones for this moment.

OTHER BOOKS WRITTEN BY
THEODORE POTTER

THE SHIPLEYS

TRUE TALES OF ALASKA AND
THEODORE POTTER'S MEMIORS

GUNS, GOLD AND TRUE LOVE

WILDSTREAK

Ebooks Available At
http://www.smashwords.com/profile/view/Potterhouse

www.ingramcontent.com/pod-product-compliance
Lightning Source LLC
Chambersburg PA
CBHW061304110426
42742CB00012BA/2056